THE VINTAGE MODERN HOME

THE VINTAGE MODERN HOME

KATHERINE SORRELL

MERRELL
LONDON · NEW YORK

PRINCIPLES
13

ESSENTIALS
89

DIRECTORY
184

Real-life homes: messy, mismatching, not quite finished, and definitely not like the pictures you see in glossy magazines. But the good news is that you *can* get the look you want, even the look of one of those glossy-magazine homes, and it's not too difficult to achieve.

I can't promise that it will be free, or plain sailing all the way (the less you're prepared to spend, the more effort you'll have to put in; that's just the way it goes), but it needn't be horribly expensive, and it's certainly not impossible.

In real life we rarely, if ever, start with a blank canvas. Instead, the problem is almost always this: how best to combine furnishings from different sources and in different styles? An old Welsh dresser, a 1950s chair, a chain-store coffee table, a junk-shop chest of drawers: we all have these diverse bits and pieces. Some of them we love; others perhaps wouldn't be our first choice, but we need to make the most of them. If you know what I mean, read on. Because whether your furnishings are precious antiques, second-hand discoveries, auction bargains or high-street pieces, this book will demonstrate how to make vintage and modern, antique and contemporary, cheap and precious work together to create a gorgeous, liveable, functional, comfortable and characterful home.

What's more, this is not just another book that's all about spending lots of money to achieve a luxury look. I take a down-to-earth attitude to decorating, and my favourite ideas are those that are both chic and cheap. Why spend a fortune when you can bag a bargain? Why buy new when you can repair or update an existing piece? Although this book isn't specifically about sustainability or style on a shoestring, those subjects are considered throughout, and heaps of practical hints and tips are provided.

But while a great many of the ideas in this book are all about thrift and economy (which are always good principles on which to base a way of life, perhaps even more so in this day and age), they're also about beautiful, irresistible things. The point is that these ideas are not incompatible. The Vintage/Modern vibe is eclectic, individual and always interesting. The cheapest touches, cleverly done, can be the most delectable. And, by following this philosophy, you can free up enough cash to splash out on one or two fabulous pieces that really make a statement, adding an incomparable element of luxury and high-end style.

The first section of the book, Principles, takes an overview of decorating in a Vintage/Modern way, looking at styles, colour, pattern and texture, small and large rooms, how to plan a room and ways to combine and contrast different elements, among other areas. These considerations form the foundation of any good decorative scheme, but here they're applied specifically to the idea of mixing old and new successfully. The second section, Basics, looks at what to buy and where to buy it, as well as how to make and repair things yourself. These vital skills for the Vintage/Modern look include bagging a bargain from a chain store and bidding for an antique at auction. The third section, Essentials, is devoted to the key elements of any scheme, from wallcoverings to flooring and from lighting to fabric, looking at the nitty-gritty of what works best for a Vintage/Modern home. It also discusses the two rooms that are probably the trickiest to tackle: kitchens and bathrooms. It is indispensable reading for anyone planning to update either of these significant spaces.

Finally, an amazing selection of real rooms demonstrates with exceptional flair how the Vintage/Modern look can work well all around the home. The owners have created exciting, appealing and – most notably – highly personal spaces, many of them on the most miniscule of budgets. These rooms may include elements of posh traditional or bold modern, subtle classic or kitsch retro, but they all have a certain humanity that an all-one-look scheme lacks completely. This sumptuous section of case studies is packed with brilliant ideas for anyone considering a Vintage/Modern scheme.

Once you've chosen the Vintage/Modern style, the first thing to learn is patience. Quick fixes *can* be the answer, but not often. Searching for the right piece for the right place may take time, but when you find it, the pleasure is all the greater for the wait. Do your research. Whether you're going to a car boot sale, specialist auction or classic design shop, or for a jaunt down the high street, you need to know what's available where and how much it's likely to cost. Acquire some practical skills: being able to sand, paint, hammer and sew will stand you in very good stead. And be prepared. I never leave the house without a pencil, notepad and tape measure in my handbag: you never know when they might be handy.

Lastly, keep an open mind. Don't be hindered by convention. Not everything has to match, or be fitted, or be brand spanking new, or conform to anything else that costs a lot of money yet ends up being a little bit boring. The joy of the Vintage/Modern home is that it follows no hard-and-fast rules, but instead makes the best of what you already have, what you can afford to buy and what you can repair or make yourself, in order to create a home that's individual, imaginative and inspiring.

PRINCIPLES

ASSESSING WHAT YOU HAVE

I make no apologies for starting this book with a number of questions: the Vintage/Modern way of life is all about thoughtfulness and patience.

Rushing in won't get you anywhere, whereas sitting down and having a think is always a good idea. First things first. I assume you have a mishmash of unrelated furnishings – family hand-me-downs, junk-shop bargains, high-street pieces, auction buys, some prized possessions, and so on – that you'd like to pull together to make a gorgeously eye-catching, fashionable and very liveable decorative scheme, without spending a fortune. The good news is that this is easily done. But before you can make any changes, you must work out where you're starting from, taking one room at a time.

So, here goes. How big is the room? Is it spacious or does it feel cramped? How well does it function, and is it comfortable? Have you too much furniture, too little, or just about the right amount? Is there enough seating, storage and lighting? How does the room

Page 15: A wall covered with photographs, postcards and old prints in coordinating frames makes a special display.

Left: A mixture of cheap retro, everyday and junk-shop items gives this kitchen an unpretentious yet stylish charm.

Below: Transparent furniture coordinates with almost any style. This simple acrylic coffee table, for example, is both cheap and practical, and works well with a decorative rug and colourful cushions.

work as a whole – which furnishings look happy in each other's company, and do they complement the walls, floor and general architecture of the house? What do you need more of? What should you get rid of? What could be updated, renovated, customized or improved? What's your budget? And what's your timescale?

Happily, this whirlwind of questions often results in fairly straightforward answers. You probably will need to get rid of some pieces, either because they're not practical in that particular space or because they just don't look all that great. Some can be put to good use elsewhere in your home, while others might have to be given away. If you're lucky, you'll be able to sell a few pieces to finance the purchase of a better-looking or more functional alternative. And you may find that, using a few simple DIY skills, you can bring about some spectacular improvements, from walls to windows, furniture to fabric. The following chapters provide much more detail on all these topics and more, and will help you make the Vintage/Modern look work in your home.

CONSIDERING STYLE

Rooms that are decorated in one particular 'style' can look utterly gorgeous. On the other hand, they may look a little obsessive, even rather like a museum.

This book is not about decorating in just one style, however. Since we're working on the basis that you're trying to make the best use of the disparate things around you, this is all about how to make two or more different styles work together with both subtlety and flair.

You don't have to be a design historian to understand style, but it is worth spending a little time considering the different styles and working out which best describe your home and its furnishings. First, there are historical styles, which can be broadly summed up as pre-eighteenth century, Georgian, Victorian, Art Deco, 1950s,

1960s/1970s, and contemporary. Then there are 'global' styles, which include English country, American Shaker, Scandinavian and the rather loosely termed 'ethnic'. Of course, some furnishings are very obviously in one particular style (think Shaker peg rails or 1950s sideboards), while others – regardless of their date or place of origin – are more anonymous (a plain pine table or a drum-shaped lampshade, say). Either one style in particular or a selection of these less showy pieces provides the backbone of most people's decorative schemes, sprinkled with an assortment of items from other places or eras.

While I'm not a fan of hard-and-fast decorating rules, there is one really useful guideline: be very careful when mixing two or more styles that are each highly elaborate or eye-catching, since it's all too easy to end up with a hideous clash. The elegance of Georgian style, the simplicity of Shaker and the pure lines of Scandinavian mean that they will all work pretty easily with other styles. Dark and heavy Victorian, chintzy English country and bold, colourful 1960s styles, on the other hand, are trickier to combine with others. On the whole, it is best to use such styles sparingly, in conjunction with understated pieces, to create interest and impact without overwhelming.

Right, top: Most early English furniture is ornate, dark and heavy. It's a strong look, so if it's for you, take care how you combine these pieces with other styles.

Right, bottom: This folk-inspired look, with tongue-and-groove panelling and decorative tilework, combines nicely with the simple lines of a 1950s plywood chair.

Previous page: This Scandinavian/mid-century Modern room, with simple, classic furniture and lighting, feels bright and airy.

20

WORKING WITH COLOUR

If you are faced with tired, mismatching or simply not-quite-right rooms, a deft use of colour is often the solution.

On everything from walls to floors and from furniture to fabrics, colour makes an immediate statement, creating atmosphere and adding personality. Colour also refreshes and updates, disguises flaws and highlights desirable features. And, perhaps most significantly for our purposes, colour is supremely good at unifying disparate elements.

Left: The most nondescript (and cheap) of wooden kitchen chairs can be transformed with a coat of bright paint.

Opposite, top: Carefully chosen fabric complements the colour of the panelling behind.

Opposite, bottom: Scarlet woodwork is fresh, bold and vivid, and works perfectly in a pared-down room.

Reaching for the paintbrush is often the answer. In a bedroom, for example, you might have a modern timber-framed bed, a reproduction chest of drawers and a faux Victorian wardrobe. The different timbers clash and the different styles simply won't talk to one another, but after a quick sand down and a brush over with a pot of ivory satinwood paint, the look is unified and considered, and an ideal starting point for highlights of colour or pattern.

Colour does not involve just paint, of course. If you have an armchair or sofa that needs re-covering, your choice of fabric colour could set the tone for the entire room. The same goes for the junk-shop tablecloth that disguises a battered dining table, or the duvet on an otherwise unremarkable spare bed. Everything, from walls and floors to accessories, makes a difference, so it's hardly surprising that choosing colours can seem tricky. But don't worry: it's not as complicated as you might think.

First, consider which colour ranges you naturally prefer, and which work best with the furnishings you already have. Do your

Opposite, top left: Bright red is vibrant and joyful but makes a strong statement. Here, it's tempered by a cool white background.

Opposite, top right: This cheerful combination of blue and green is perfect for a country cottage.

Opposite, bottom: Touches of red and blue, set off by pale green walls, give a happy, retro vibe.

Right: This elegant shade of green is typically Georgian. The contrasting twentieth-century furniture has been kept neutral in colour, so that the two styles complement each other.

favoured colours feel right with the architecture of the property? 'Historic', muted colours sometimes work best in older houses, for example. And do your colours show off the spaces to their best advantage? Pale colours increase the feeling of spaciousness, while darker colours absorb light and therefore appear more enclosing and cosy. These considerations, and practical ones, too (you may need a dark-painted hallway, for example, to cope with the scrapes and splashes of family life), are an obvious starting point. Look for ideas in other people's houses and in books and magazines, shop windows, restaurants, films, your garden – anywhere, in fact, that you find inspirational. Then experiment with different combinations, using fabric swatches and sample pots, considering which colours work together, how they relate from room to room, and the way they change in different lights. Developing an 'eye' for colour is a marvellous thing, and whether you decide on bold, bright shades or subtle, sophisticated neutrals, a clever use of colour could be the key to success in your interior scheme.

USING PATTERN

Pattern, like colour, can be a
wonderful addition to a home,
providing character and vitality.

Pattern can create a focal point: think of the impact of re-covering
a tatty old armchair in an oversized print, for example. A few simple
pieces with charming, understated designs can provide subtle
interest. Or pattern can be the *raison d'être* of an entire room,
in a complex combination of patterned walls, rugs, fabrics and
accessories. And when you are putting together disparate furnishings
for a Vintage/Modern scheme, pattern – whether in the form
of elegant antiques, bold retro pieces or pared-down modern
items – will almost always feature.

We all have our own pattern preferences. For every one of us who loves delicate florals, there's someone else who can't get enough of bold, modern abstracts, and while for many people, such subtle patterns as spots or stripes are ideal, others aren't afraid to go the whole hog with flamboyant designs. A limited touch of pattern to break the monotony of an otherwise plain room? An eye-caching overall look? A clever compromise employing, perhaps, one wall of patterned paper or a few upholstered pieces? As I say, we're all different.

There's no denying that it's easier to follow the simple route with pattern, and limit it to just one or two occurrences. But combining a variety of patterns, although harder to get right, can be tremendously exciting and create great impact. Whatever patterned items you're putting together, there are some guidelines that will help make the best of them. First, match colours precisely: they will

Previous page, top:
A trailing damask
patterned paper has
been used for a 'feature
wall' in this elegant
bedroom, providing
a subtly decorative
contrast to the plain
and striped fabrics.

Previous page, bottom:
Patterned cushions
are ideal for adding
interest and can be
as understated or as
dramatic as you like.

Left, top and bottom:
Kitchens tend to
be relatively plain,
simple places, and
incorporating patterned
tiles as splashbacks is a
great way to introduce
vigour and vitality.

unify any pattern scheme. Secondly, think about scale. In general, bigger patterns are better suited to bigger rooms, and smaller patterns to cosier rooms, although there's something to be said for the occasional use of a huge pattern as a focal point in a small space. Avoid dramatic changes of scale, which tend to look strange. Thirdly, steer clear of an incongruous mix of patterns from different eras or aesthetics. A delicate Georgian floral is unlikely to sit well with a 1970s abstract geometric, for example, but will look wonderful when combined with another pretty, spriggy floral of any origin. Remember that stripes coordinate brilliantly with more intricate patterns. And fourthly, cheat! If you love the idea of pattern but are really stuck, look at manufacturers' wallpaper and fabric pattern books, which show you how to mix and match with ease. Keep experimenting and persevere. Success with pattern is simply a case of trial and error, putting different things together and changing them around until you're totally happy with the result.

THE IMPORTANCE OF TEXTURE

Colours and patterns are likely to be the first things you notice when you walk into a room, but after spending a little time in it, you'll find that textures, too, become significant.

Both obviously and subliminally, textures enhance your sense of comfort and ease, as well as providing visual interest and tactile appeal. Vintage, worn and pre-loved pieces come into their own here: knitting, crochet, lace and quilting; distressed or varnished wood; woven willow; worn stone; polished chrome; foxed mirror … the possibilities are endless.

Left: This polished concrete floor contrasts beautifully with timber panelling and exposed bricks.

Below: The attractive grain of smooth, natural timber makes a pleasing textural foil for a ruffle of gingham.

Opposite: A shaggy throw, smooth floorboards, a hairy rug, flat paintwork and rough bricks: this room contains nothing but neutral colours, yet has it all in terms of textural ingredients.

Think of this aspect of room design as using the layering of textures to provide pleasing contrasts. It may sound challenging, but in fact it's as natural as placing a woven rug on smooth floorboards, edging a woollen blanket with silk satin or piling a plain cotton sofa with embroidered cushions. Textures involve just about every aspect of a room, from size and lighting to colour schemes and style. To bring out the cosiness of a small bedroom, for example, you could combine a fluffy rug, matt-painted walls, velvet curtains and chintzy quilts. Or, to emphasize the brightness and airiness of a living room, the main features might be varnished floorboards, glossy white woodwork, sheer curtains and glass or chrome lamp bases: lovely and absolutely not difficult – especially when you're combining old and new pieces. In fact, it soon becomes easy to see how a considered use of texture can underpin a scheme, bringing vintage and modern together beautifully.

THE SIGNIFICANCE OF SIZE AND SCALE

Convenient though it would be to think that combining vintage and modern is always easy, unfortunately that isn't necessarily the case.

Putting together disparate items of furniture, in particular, can be tricky, and one of the problems concerns size and scale. Pieces that are very different in size and proportion tend to look odd together, no matter what else they have in common. It starts with practicality – dining chairs need to be of a useable height for the table around which they're placed, for example – but also refers to visual impact and overall style. In a living room with two sofas, say, if one is very heavy and overstuffed, while the other is low, lean and slender, they will not work all that well as a pair.

Previous page: The grandeur of oversized furnishings makes a big (pardon the pun) statement. Here, they work because the room is sparsely furnished and each piece is exceptional in its own right.

Right: Similar scales, simple forms and strong horizontal lines – all at the same height – help this room feel cool, calm and collected.

The trick is, first, to relate the size of the furnishings to one another: a huge antique table needs solid-looking chairs rather than delicate, spindly ones; a low, lean sofa is better matched with a similarly proportioned coffee table; a grand four-poster bed will work best with relatively large bedside tables. Also, perhaps less obviously, it's good to choose furnishings that work with the overall size of the room (of which more later), and that incorporate features of similar scale: the depth of carving on a chair-back, the size of the knob on a cupboard door or the height of feet on a sideboard, for example. Bearing this in mind may require you to hunt around junk shops or markets for a little longer in search of the perfect vintage find, or it could mean making minor modifications to pieces you already have. But it's worth it. When pieces are of different styles, originate from different periods or are made from a range of materials, their differences and similarities become vital, and can determine whether you create a scheme that looks and feels odd, or one that's eclectic but stylish and comfortable.

SMALL ROOMS

Small rooms are often seen as a problem, but they do have certain advantages.

Having less room for furniture may mean that there's more cash to spend on each piece, and will perhaps give you the chance to choose a higher-quality finish overall. Also, the extra time you'll need to spend on planning is likely to result in a space that works very efficiently. The result? A small but perfectly formed room that could well be the most appealing place in your home.

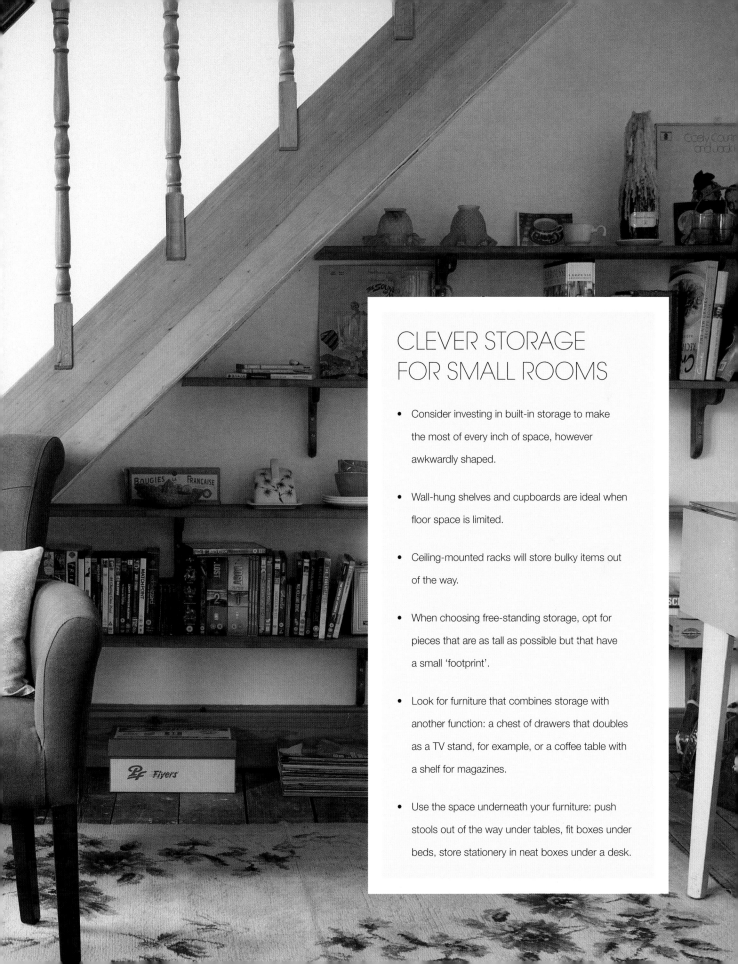

CLEVER STORAGE FOR SMALL ROOMS

- Consider investing in built-in storage to make the most of every inch of space, however awkwardly shaped.

- Wall-hung shelves and cupboards are ideal when floor space is limited.

- Ceiling-mounted racks will store bulky items out of the way.

- When choosing free-standing storage, opt for pieces that are as tall as possible but that have a small 'footprint'.

- Look for furniture that combines storage with another function: a chest of drawers that doubles as a TV stand, for example, or a coffee table with a shelf for magazines.

- Use the space underneath your furniture: push stools out of the way under tables, fit boxes under beds, store stationery in neat boxes under a desk.

LOVE SONNY

Previous page: Using the space under the stairs is a classic trick, whether it's for shelving, as here, a miniature study, built-in cupboards or even an extra loo or shower room.

Left: Make a small room feel grand and exciting by using bold colours and strong patterns.

The rules for small rooms are fairly straightforward. First, don't overcrowd – keep the number of items in the room to a minimum; and secondly, don't overwhelm – avoid furnishings that are too tall, too bulky or too busy for the space. This means that you may need to steer clear of Victorian or Edwardian pieces, many of which were built to a rather imposing scale and feature decorative twiddles that are just too ornate. Georgian furniture, on the other hand, is usually more delicate, while the low, lean lines of retro furnishings are particularly suited to small or low-ceilinged rooms. Much contemporary furniture, too, is not only spare in form but also cleverly designed to enable you to make the most of limited space:

wheeled, folding or hideaway pieces, compact furnishings and dual-purpose items, such as sofa beds or storage seats. Bear in mind that furniture raised on legs – whether a sofa, kitchen cupboard or bath – will, by increasing the visible floor area, make the room seem larger, as will furniture that is transparent (it could be made of glass, acrylic or wire) or reflective (made of metal or mirror).

Thinking beyond furniture, get clever with colour, choosing pale, airy shades to enhance the feeling of space; add small-scale patterns on a pale, open background. And finally, maximize light by keeping window treatments minimal and adding an interesting variety of table and floor lamps.

Convention says that small rooms should be painted white to make the most of the space, and patterns kept light and delicate. But sometimes it just works better to emphasize the cosy nature of the tiny space, using deep colours and vibrant patterns, as here.

LARGE ROOMS

Wonderfully huge, bright and airy
open spaces are what we'd all love
to have at home, but whether you've
got a multi-purpose, open-plan living
area or simply want to make the
most of a spacious room, careful
planning is still important.

To start with, it makes sense, where possible, to use big furnishings and larger-scale patterns that won't be dwarfed by their environment. All this should be within reason, of course; don't go all 'Alice in Wonderland' by using giant furnishings that only very tall people will feel comfortable with. Ceiling height is another factor to consider: high-backed furniture (antique or modern) and large pictures or wall hangings will look great in high-ceilinged spaces. It's also worth bearing in mind that conventional light-fittings can look like pimples in large rooms with high ceilings, so be bold and choose fittings that seem oversized. Once they're up, they'll look very impressive.

When positioning furniture, don't make the classic mistake of placing it all at the edges of the room. Avoid the nursing-home look and instead create zones – for reading, watching TV, working, whatever – by grouping furniture comfortably. You may want to place a pair of sofas or a set of free-standing shelves, for example, in such a way that they break up the floor area into useable chunks. The clever use of flooring will help, too, whether it's a change of material between 'zones', or simply the judicious use of a rug or two in appropriate places. Employ colour and pattern to reinforce the different areas within the room – perhaps a wallpapered wall beside a cosy reading corner, or a subtle range of paint colours that contrast one area of the room with another – and, lastly, try to ensure that your lighting scheme is flexible enough to provide both strong lighting where necessary and soft ambience when wanted.

Page 41: The massive lampshade, large armchair and huge artwork all draw attention to the spaciousness of this converted loft.

Opposite, top: Tall, slender vases are a great option when you have double-height ceilings.

Opposite, bottom: Groupings of furniture and the placing of rugs divide this huge room into comfortably useable areas.

Right: Imposing light-fittings are ideal for spaces with high ceilings; in fact, anything smaller could look twee.

PLANNING A SCHEME

There are so many elements involved in the design of a room, particularly when your aim is to achieve an attractive Vintage/Modern mix, that it's worth spending some time on the nitty-gritty of planning.

First, measure the room and draw a plan as accurately as you can (using graph paper makes it easier), marking existing windows, doors, built-in cupboards, radiators, plug sockets, light-fittings and so on. Do you need to move a wall or radiator, enlarge a window, hang a door the other way round or add sockets? In bathrooms and kitchens you'll need to work out where the existing pipework (if any) is run, and whether that needs to be altered.

If the structure is satisfactory, consider the room's size and shape, and its architectural style. How will they affect the way in which you decorate? Are there special considerations, such as a lack of space or the presence of a particular original feature, with which you must work?

Now go back to the graph paper. It's time to work out how to arrange your furniture. Sketch on to a separate sheet (but at the same scale) the approximate shapes of your furnishings, as if you were looking at them from above, and cut them out. Place them on your masterplan and assess how well they fit into the space, moving them around as necessary, and allowing adequate room for activity between and around them. Eventually, it will all fall into place and bingo! – you've got the basis of a functional, comfortable room.

Making a sample board

To ensure that all the decorative elements of a room work together, professional designers create a 'sample board'. Simply take a large piece of neutral-coloured card as a base, and stick to it small pieces of your chosen fabrics, wallpaper and flooring, and paint swatches. If possible, add photographs or sketches of furnishings, light-fittings and other elements. It's important to keep the samples in proportion to the size they'll be in real life, so that a curtain fabric swatch is much larger than, say, one representing a cushion; it also helps if you place the samples roughly in accordance with their place in the room: floorings at the bottom, curtain fabrics near the top and furnishings in the middle. When the board is finished, you can assess the overall effect and correct any mistakes before it's too late.

Use manufacturers' paint charts to help you choose colours that coordinate. A good tip is to select swatches from the same row, either horizontally or vertically, as they will work well together.

AN ECLECTIC MIX

A mix of Vintage/Modern pieces can be full of impact, creating drama and interest through the surprising juxtaposition of different styles and eras. But before you pile all your stuff in one room, think carefully. Following a few basic guidelines will help avoid the badly arranged-junkshop look that is, unfortunately, all too easy to achieve when aiming for this style.

Until now I've talked about how to use style, colour, pattern, texture and scale when creating a Vintage/Modern scheme. Now's your chance to work with all these elements at once. Don't be afraid to move things around or, generally, to be highly selective. 'If in doubt, take it out' should be your golden rule here.

A common mistake is to have too many 'star' pieces. Rather than demonstrating your amazing good taste in owning so many lovely things, this is distracting and doesn't produce an attractive scheme. Two or three 'wow-factor' items are quite enough, and the rest can be 'subtle but interesting'. Aim to establish a subliminal link between the room's disparate contents, perhaps through the use of colour, pattern or texture, via similarities of style or size, or with some other theme that creates a striking but coherent and desirable overall effect.

Previous page: While every piece is full of character, the colours are subtly coordinated and the scales well related – with the exception of the blue lamp, which is made to stand out as the star of the show.

Above: There is no reason why you shouldn't combine a large gilt letter with a Victorian chest of drawers and modern wallpaper. They look fabulous here.

Opposite: A monochrome colour palette unifies an eclectic selection of furnishings.

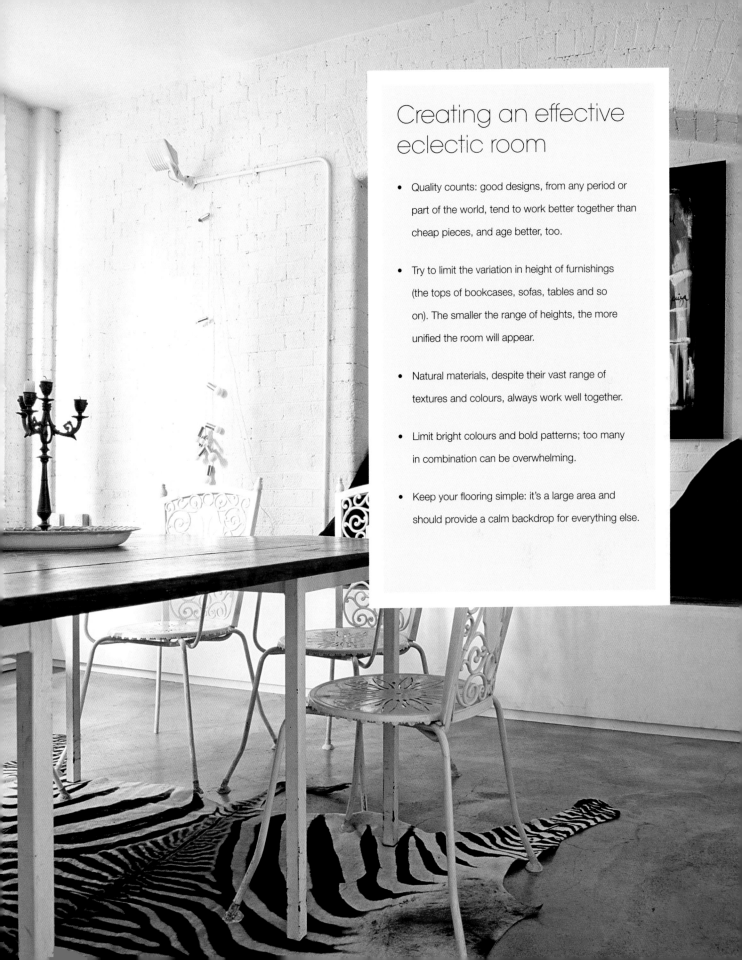

Creating an effective eclectic room

- Quality counts: good designs, from any period or part of the world, tend to work better together than cheap pieces, and age better, too.

- Try to limit the variation in height of furnishings (the tops of bookcases, sofas, tables and so on). The smaller the range of heights, the more unified the room will appear.

- Natural materials, despite their vast range of textures and colours, always work well together.

- Limit bright colours and bold patterns; too many in combination can be overwhelming.

- Keep your flooring simple: it's a large area and should provide a calm backdrop for everything else.

DRAMATIC JUXTAPOSITION

One of the easiest ways to create a fabulous Vintage/Modern impression is to contrast either the architecture of your home or the style of most of its furnishings with a few key pieces that are dramatically different.

Just think of the fab juxtaposition of a Georgian house and classic twentieth-century furniture; or a country cottage with Scandinavian furniture; or a home that contains ultra-modern items offset by one or two breathtaking antiques.

The main reason this look is so effective is that when everything matches it's just a little … boring. Breaking up the careful coordination produces a joyful, even somewhat naughty thrill. And it works for all budgets. Owners of period homes and classic designer furniture, search no further: your look is right here. But even if your home is architecturally indifferent, and furnished largely with middle-of-the-road contemporary pieces, you can still create a bold, brave contrast without digging too deep into your pockets. How about finishing off that chain-store sofa with cushions made from fragments of retro fabrics? Or adding a Victorian pine wall cupboard to that bland, contemporary kitchen? Or putting a classic hinged-arm lamp on your new bedside table?

Grand antiques make
an exciting contrast with
the pared-down lines of
modern architecture.

Although the aim is to create a contrast, it's still important to consider the similarities between two apparently diverse looks. The reason Georgian architecture and modern furniture go so well together, for example, is that both have a pleasingly spare aesthetic; that pine cupboard will look good in a modern kitchen only if it's hung at the same level as other wall units, creating a unified line, and only if its colour coordinates with others used elsewhere in the room; and perhaps that chrome lamp picks up the metal handles of the chest of drawers. These are subtle details, but even when the big picture is one of drama and wham-bam impact, it's these details that make that picture truly effective and appealing.

Opposite: A space-age
'Tulip' dining table and
chairs from the 1960s
are placed in a modern
industrial setting.
The curvy lines of the
furniture are a foil for
the harsh linearity
of the room.

Right: A lovely contrast
of rococo carving and
simple typography. Both
white-painted wood,
they work wonderfully
against each other.

BASICS

SECOND-HAND STYLE

Pre-owned, pre-loved, nearly
new and not-in-the-slightest-bit-new
furnishings are readily available
almost everywhere, making second-
hand style a snip to achieve. When it
comes to deciding where to buy, it's
best to be open-minded: it's not the
venue that matters, after all, but what
is being sold. Opposite are some
ideas to start with.

Flea markets
Car boot sales
Auction rooms
Private dealers
Junk shops
Salvage yards
Jumble sales
Antiques fairs
Charity shops
Small ads in the
    local newspaper
The Internet

The biggest problem with second-hand style is that, unless you're looking for very readily available pieces, there's a certain amount of karma involved in getting exactly what you want. Obviously, the harder you look and the wider you cast your net, the more likely you are to succeed in your search, but nevertheless you may have to be patient and/or compromise. 'Thinking outside the box' is what this look is all about, after all, so if you go out looking for a lampshade and come home with a Lloyd Loom chair, what the heck. Just make sure you really want or need the piece you're buying, and that it's well made, will function appropriately and will – even if it takes a bit of tinkering – look good in your home.

Another excellent piece of advice is (just like the Boy Scouts) to be prepared. If you're on the lookout for anything to which size makes a difference, whether it's a roll-top bath or a chest of drawers, make a list of the relevant dimensions and keep it, together with a mini tape measure, on your person at all times. You might also consider carrying tiny swatches of fabric, chips of paint colour, snaps of your rooms and furniture, and even pages torn from magazines that inspire you – anything that helps. That way you won't get caught out when the perfect, stylish second-hand item comes your way.

Previous page:
Second-hand shops
are wonderful to
browse around and can
yield fantastic finds.

Opposite: The term
'second-hand' can
encompass anything
from antiques to
jumble-sale buys.
It's not the name
that matters, but how
useful and attractive
your find will be to you.

Buying at auction

Salerooms have regular 'general' or 'household' auctions of second-hand furnishings and effects: everything from sofas and rugs to wardrobes, chests of drawers, linen, mirrors and even electrical equipment. Lots can be cheap as chips, and buying is not nearly as scary as you might think.

1   Check catalogues or go online to find potential bargains. If appropriate, try to go to a viewing, or request a condition report. You can't get a refund if you make a mistake and your 'good deal' turns out to be a dud.

2   Register to bid with the saleroom. You may need to provide identification and/or your bank details.

3   When you arrive, you'll usually be issued with a numbered paddle, which you raise when you wish to bid. (Don't worry: scratching your nose won't make you bid by accident!) Many salerooms allow you to bid by phone or online, or by placing an absentee bid in advance.

4   If you win the lot, you'll pay the 'hammer price' (the amount of your bid) plus a buyer's premium and any applicable taxes. Often, you're obliged to pay immediately, so find out in advance what payment methods are acceptable, and have cash, a chequebook or a credit card with you.

5   You may be able to take your purchase home with you straight away. Alternatively, arrange to collect it later or have it delivered to you.

FURNISHING FOR FREE

It doesn't matter whether you're on a tight budget or just love a bargain: why pay for furniture when you can get it free?

And no, I'm not talking about inheriting the family antiques – although of course that is a tried-and-tested means of acquiring furniture without paying for it – but about rather more proactive methods. So, how do you go about getting something for nothing? Well, first you could try skip-dipping or dumpster-diving – the fine art of removing unwanted items from other people's skips. Many a desirable piece, from floorboards to kitchen cupboards, has been rehomed in this way, and it's as easy as pie, particularly if you bring a step to stand on, some heavy-duty gloves and perhaps a pole with a hook on the end. There are just two rules: never trespass, and always ask the owner's permission before taking anything.

That's the traditional method. A more twenty-first-century approach involves simply signing up to an Internet-based network (such as Freecycle) that connects people who don't want things any more with people who will happily take them off their hands. You won't get a designer piece, but if you need something basic this is the ideal solution. It's generally hassle-free, but there is an etiquette: try to give away something for every item you receive. If nothing else, it's just good karma. It's not unheard-of to find unwanted furnishings (sometimes pretty good ones) out on the street, perhaps next to a rubbish bin or a skip, or simply left on the corner. As long as you're certain their owners no longer want them, they're yours for the taking, although you should check carefully that they're not damaged, full of woodworm or otherwise problematic. Another approach, if you have either unwanted furnishings or handy skills, is to swap or barter with family or friends or, again, via an online community. In all these scenarios, the chances are that you'll have to get out the screwdriver or paintbrush to repair, refurbish or otherwise 'upcycle' your new acquisition, but at least your wallet won't feel any the lighter, and you'll have the satisfaction of knowing that your new furniture has been rescued from landfill and given a useful new life.

Sometimes you'll come across old furniture left out on the street. Make absolutely certain no one wants it before you take it, though.

61

MAKE DO, MEND ... AND IMPROVE

No matter how clumsy you think you are, it's worth mustering up some basic DIY skills in order to make the most of broken, old or simply boring furnishings. Not only will you save money, but also you can be wonderfully smug about having done it all with your own fair hands.

Both basic repairs and, happily, a great deal of what is now fashionably known as 'upcycling' or 'repurposing' can be very easy. For example, one of my favourite ways to improve an old piece of furniture is to change its knobs or handles. Simply unscrew the old ones, attach their replacements (if the old holes aren't in the right places, you may have to fill them and make new ones) and *voilà* – a transformation. Another lovely idea is to use patterned self-adhesive plastic inside old chests or wardrobes, creating not only a smooth lining for clothes, but also a jolly surprise every time the door or drawer is opened. It's possible to paste wallpaper (or wrapping paper, maps, sheet music, posters – whatever you like) on to the flat panels of wooden furniture, painting the rest of the piece in a coordinating colour, to give it a quirky makeover. If you can handle a saw, you could even up the legs of a wobbly chair, or shorten those

of an unwanted dining table to turn it into a coffee table. Glue mirror tiles or sheet mirror to wardrobe doors; staple a new fabric cover over a removable dining-chair seat pad; rub candle wax on drawer runners to make them open more smoothly; re-cover a headboard in boldly patterned fabric …

Whether you need to bring a dodgy piece of furniture up to scratch or enhance its looks overall, you will need ingenuity and the willingness to have a go, rather than advanced capabilities. The exception, of course, is when the furniture is very valuable, rare or old. In that case, don't even think about attempting a makeover; undertake essential repairs only, and ensure you get it right by either attending a specialist course or entrusting the work to a professional.

Left: With a can-do attitude, you'll easily be able to re-cane a chair seat, level a wonky table or change the handles on cabinet furniture. They will look as good as new.

Overleaf: Tools need good storage, and nothing beats a set of hooks or nails for keeping them out of the way. If you happen to have a vintage 'weekly planner', so much the better.

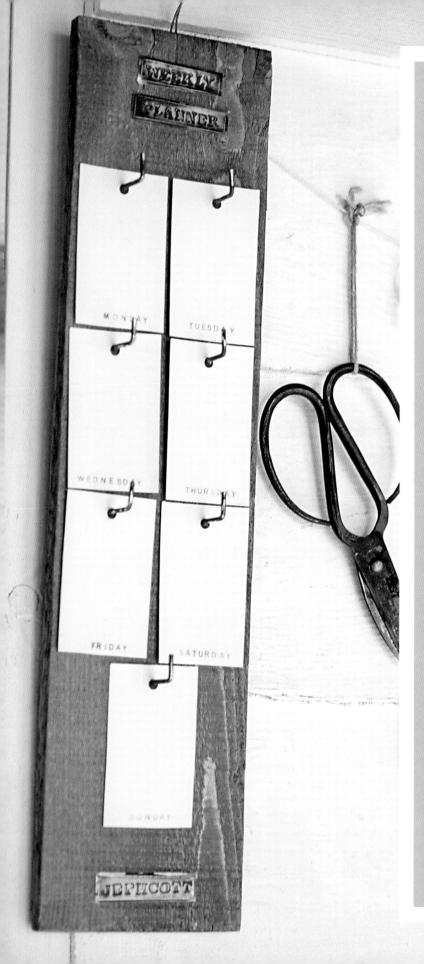

A basic tool set

This list will get you started, and you'll inevitably add to it as you tackle different projects. Get the best you can afford; it's a false economy to buy cheap kit. However, it's usually cheaper to hire power tools than to buy them, unless you plan to use them regularly.

Extending tape measure and pencil

Sandpaper in a variety of grades

Filler and filling knife

Scrapers for wallpaper and paint

Wire brush

Cloths (cut up old sheets, T-shirts and other
    unwanted fabric)

Paintbrushes in a variety of sizes

Paint roller and tray

Proprietary brush cleaner

Set of screwdrivers and Allen keys

Medium-weight hammer

Tenon saw

Hacksaw

Spirit level

Cutting knife

Large scissors

Pasting brush

Electric drill and a range of bits

Adjustable spanner

Clamp

Staple gun

Pliers

Dust sheets

Masking tape

Protective goggles and gloves

Compartmentalized toolbox with handle

A LICK OF PAINT

When it comes to DIY, I'm all for the easy option, and it doesn't get much easier than simply picking up a paintbrush.

You can use paint to accentuate the individuality of your home, to provide a neutral background for special furnishings, to unify disparate possessions or simply to revive and restore almost anything you like. It's cheap, too, and the results are both instant and dramatic. What's not to like?

Nothing transforms a room more quickly than a coat of paint on the walls, whether you're freshening up with clean, bright white or introducing an interesting colour. A slightly more arduous option, but still not beyond the scope of a novice, is to paint a wooden floor that's seen better days. I like white for an ethereal and airy look (it will show a bit of wear, but you'll have to accept that as part of the charm) or glossy black for a smart look that goes with anything (it hides the dirt, too, and – contrary to what you might think – doesn't make the room too dark).

When it comes to architectural features – skirtings, door frames, cornices and the like – a great tip is to use a slightly darker tone for the woodwork than for the walls. If you have dado rails, you may wish to vary the wall tones, with a lighter one above and a darker one below the division. Bear in mind that halls, stairways

Above, left: Vivid colours transform a room, and can easily be painted over if you tire of them.

Above, right: Simple wooden chairs, not necessarily matching in style or shape, are the perfect candidates for a paint job.

Opposite: A pale wall looks calm and fresh, is easy to live with and makes an excellent backdrop for other neutrals or stronger shades.

Painting wooden furniture

Before you start, do any necessary repairs and remove any drawers, doors, handles and knobs.

1 Use medium-grade sandpaper to rub the piece down thoroughly, then wipe it with a damp cloth.

2 If you're painting bare wood, you'll need a coat of primer first. Otherwise, paint on a layer of undercoat. If that hasn't covered the base colour well enough, add another coat. For a really professional finish, rub down between each coat with wet-and-dry sandpaper and water.

3 Finish with a top coat of eggshell, satin or gloss paint, depending on the level of shine you want.

4 Leave to dry thoroughly, then re-attach all the fittings.

and landings are linking areas. When you stand in them you may be able to see a number of different rooms, so you should consider how their colours will work together: perhaps a very pale colour in a narrow hallway, with slightly darker hues in a living room and a warm tone in a dining room, for example.

As for furnishings, well, paint is the obvious option for the Vintage/Modern look. A worn or not particularly attractive piece of furniture, for example, can be given a new lease of life with either a quick lick of white or off-white paint for a neutral, barely-there appearance, or something braver to make a bold statement. Imagine a 1950s sideboard repainted with lime-green gloss, or a set of DIY-store garden chairs painted in ice-cream pastel shades. A paint job is ideal for a junk-shop find or an old or cheap chain-store purchase – although obviously not for valuable antiques. Tables and chairs, cabinets and sideboards, wardrobes and chests of drawers, even built-in shelves and cupboards – not to mention small accessories, such as lamp bases, mirror frames, storage boxes and plant pots – can all be revamped quite easily. Inside and outdoors, paint is the perfect starting point for a creative makeover.

Painted furniture needn't be pristine: a bit of distressing can look charming and lend real character to a piece.

DESIGN CLASSICS

The twentieth century produced
some extraordinary names
in furniture design, including
Le Corbusier, Arne Jacobsen,
Alvar Aalto and Verner Panton,
and their pieces are now
sought-after classics.

Products by these masters of problem-solving and innovation are
timelessly stylish and utterly desirable. At the top of my wish list is
the Barcelona chair by Ludwig Mies van der Rohe, but I wouldn't
say no to an Eames lounge chair, a Poul Henningsen Artichoke lamp
or a Tulip dining set by Eero Saarinen. A girl can dream!

If your dream, too, is to own a twentieth-century classic, start saving now: chairs, tables, sofas and even light-fittings cost a pretty penny. Many are still in production (see the websites of Knoll, Herman Miller and Vitra listed at the back of this book for some inspirational examples), while older pieces can be found in designer auctions or at higher-end furniture dealers; but, old or new, they are sure to be accompanied by an eye-watering price tag. Classic furnishings are often as expensive as – perhaps even more than – new. And watch out: if you find a so-called classic online for what seems to be an unbelievably good price, it's probably a fake. There are plenty of 'replicas' available, some acceptable, others not so good. And while many are offered by well-intentioned companies who are completely open about their products' provenance, not all sellers are so honest. It's the old story: buyer beware, and a little research on designers and their work will be well worth the effort. If you're on a strict budget, your money is much better spent on a designer accessory – an Aalto vase, say, or an Eames wall rack – or on a piece by a young designer, perhaps one day a classic in its own right.

Classic pieces look wonderful in almost any setting; their design really does stand the test of time. Clockwise from opposite, top: Alvar Aalto's Lounge Chair 406; Ludwig Mies van der Rohe's Barcelona chair and ottoman; a lounger and ottoman by Charles and Ray Eames; Eames moulded plywood chairs; curvy 1950s-style side tables by Ercol; and Achille Castiglioni's fabulous Arco floor lamp.

PROPER ANTIQUES

What do I mean by 'proper' antiques? The strict definition is anything more than 100 years old, but for our Vintage/Modern purposes I mean eighteenth-, nineteenth- and early twentieth-century furnishings: a Victorian sofa or wardrobe, an Edwardian bath or a Georgian dining set, for example.

Previous page: A good-quality chest of drawers with a marble top makes a lovely piece of bedroom furniture, and should be well looked after.

Above: A carved, gilded and beautifully upholstered (if somewhat frayed) chair makes an elegant addition to a modern space.

Above, right: Imposing Chinese-style lanterns are a great contrast to the classic period detailing of this hallway.

Right: An upholstered antique French bed is an unadulterated luxury.

Opposite: The high-quality wood and intricate carved detailing of this dining table and chair set make it a fine example: expensive and eminently desirable.

There's no doubt that antiques add an inimitable style and character to a room, but – to my mind – a great deal of 'dark wood' furniture is simply not very attractive. What's more, it's often too large to sit well in a modern home, creating a heavy feel, rather like an overstuffed Victorian parlour. So, while it's worth seeking out one or two beautiful antique furnishings – whether dark wood or lighter, simpler pieces – to add to your eclectic mix, a cautious, minimal approach is advisable.

Some people buy antique furniture as an investment, but it's also essential to get what you like. After all, you have to live with it. Before you venture to an auction house or dealer's showroom, do a little research into the sort of pieces you're looking for; get a feel for what's out there and how much it usually costs. Think seriously, too, about how a piece will fit into your home. Old wardrobes, dining tables, dressers, sofas and chests of drawers can be bulky, so in a smallish home it might be wiser to get your antiques fix with such pieces as stools, mirrors, wall shelves or bedroom chairs. Don't forget accessories, too: crockery, cutlery, silverware, glass, tablecloths, lace and light-fittings. When buying, don't be afraid to ask (politely, of course) for a discount on the labelled price. 'What's your best price on this?' is a miraculous phrase that can turn an expensive antique into an affordable luxury that will transform your home.

GOING RETRO

Retro furnishings from the 1950s, 1960s and 1970s have a funky but nostalgic vibe that makes a lovely addition to the Vintage/Modern mix.

It's possible to pick up pieces very cheaply – at car boot sales or in second-hand shops, for instance – especially if they need a bit of TLC; on the other hand, rare or special items from these eras can cost a pretty penny, and change hands at auction or via specialist dealers. The alternative is to go for modern things made in 'retro' style: if you choose wisely they can be absolutely gorgeous.

You can easily spot a 1950s sofa by its low, slim form, upright, rectangular shape and lean, clean upholstery.

Key pieces for a touch of 1950s nostalgia include slim, low sofas or sideboards with splayed legs, fabrics with molecular or organic–abstract patterns, and kitsch accessories, such as coloured drinks tumblers, 'handkerchief' glass vases and flying ducks. From the 1960s and 1970s, look for curvy plastic furniture in bright colours, fabrics with swirly, psychedelic patterns, and spherical clocks, lamps or radios. And let's not forget fabulous American diner style, with groovy chrome, red leather and bright neon signs.

Retro furnishings are fun, lively and colourful, and will add oodles of character to an otherwise plain and laid-back room. A few well-chosen pieces will mix well with both older and newer furnishings, provided you stick to a coherent overview of shape, material, colour and pattern. From a teapot to a side table or a magazine rack to a coffee mug, the challenge of finding the loveliest vintage bargains for your home is so exciting and rewarding that you'll probably never want to stop.

Above: Marimekko's Unikko print is an enduring classic and looks just as good in a contemporary home as it did in the 1960s.

Left: This look is fabulously retro, yet still very liveable today.

Opposite: No classics here, just lovely vintage bits and pieces that have a joyful vibe and look great casually thrown together.

ON THE HIGH STREET

While high-street buys are not
always tremendously exciting,
there's no doubt that they're quick,
cheap and convenient, offering
good-value staples for any room
in a Vintage/Modern home.

Simple and inexpensive, this side table – and the two vases on it – looks perfect in this Victorian hallway. It provides useful storage, too.

When price is a factor – and after all, when isn't it? – the big names on the high street we all know and (mostly) love offer unparalleled choice without breaking the bank. The same goes for their online versions and, even less glamorous, the DIY sheds. WIth a discerning eye you can pick up some great bargains in all these places.

What should you look for? First of all, while cheap is undoubtedly tempting, the best value lies in good design and quality of manufacture. Plain pieces can be reasonably priced, well made and extremely useful, and can easily be customized or accessorized for added interest where necessary. Many high-street shops also have excellent designer diffusion ranges, offering star-name looks with affordable price tags. You'll find that everything from towels to lampshades is given a celebrity moniker, though I feel that cushions,

bedlinen and throws are particularly good buys of this type. In some high-street retailers you'll also come across furniture inspired by some of the great designer classics. It's not for purists, obviously, but if you're on a budget and yearn for a little of this look, it's a definite option.

And, on the subject of budgets, one final word: it goes without saying that sales are the high-street bargain-hunter's bonanza, but there are other ways to save when it comes to this type of shopping. You can sign up for a store card in order to get a discount, for example (you don't have to use it afterwards), take advantage of online discount codes, or visit outlet/factory/clearance stores (physically or online). Happy shopping!

CRAFTY CHIC

In case you hadn't noticed, there's a craft revival going on, and anyone who's anyone has joined a knitting circle, quilting group or sewing club.

I must confess to having been a craft addict ever since I could pick up a roll of double-sided sticky tape and attach a badly cut piece of cardboard to an old washing-up-liquid bottle. Goodness knows what I thought I was making, but the point is – why not have a go? There are a host of craft skills that are enormously helpful in putting together a Vintage/Modern look, whether it's reviving a damaged, dull or down-at-heel piece, or creating something entirely from scratch. And, quite apart from the practical, money-saving element, making (or restoring) something yourself is incredibly satisfying.

I left a little of myself at the shore

It doesn't take long to think of a huge number of ways in which a little crafty know-how can come in handy, whether it's carpentry (mending or making wooden furniture), caning (repairing sagging seats) or crochet (a snuggly throw, anyone?); knitting (how about a soft hot-water-bottle cover?) or embroidery (monogrammed cushions or napkins, perhaps); or what's probably the ultimate in terms of usefulness: machine sewing. Master that and you can run up curtains or tablecloths, seat covers or blinds at the drop of a hat. Once you get bitten by the bug you may find you want to try out all sorts of other crafts, from screen-printing to beading, and from basketry to mosaic. And why not? You're bound to be able to put whatever you've made to good use around your home.

Most craft skills are reasonably easy to get going with. Start with the simple stuff, keep practising and don't expect perfection. The point about home-made (or home-renovated) pieces is that they have unique character and charm, not the anonymous, machine-made looks of something anyone can buy cheaply on the high street. So if it's a touch wobbly, try not to worry. And remember, if you don't have all the expertise you'd like, find a how-to book in your local library, look it up on the Internet or join an evening class, because it's fashionable, fun, thrifty, green, calming and useful. Craft, in short, is cool.

Previous page: What could be more lovely than hand-stitched embroidery? So simple to do, yet so effective.

Right: The irresistible colours of these silk embroidery threads are a joy in themselves.

Opposite: Whatever you choose to make by hand, it will bring character, individuality and soul to a scheme.

Ten crafty ideas for things to make yourself at home

1   Knit or crochet squares in different colours (use leftover yarn or unravelled old jumpers) and stitch together to make a throw.

2   Use broken crockery or tiles to create a mosaic splashback for a basin.

3   Turn an old tablecloth or pair of curtains into a smart Roman blind.

4   Update a tired pair of plain curtains by stitching on a narrow border of contrasting fabric.

5   Potato-print a design with fabric paint on to plain cotton and make into dining-chair seat pads.

6   Cut out a large stencil and print the design on to lining paper for a lovely home-made alternative to wallpaper.

7   Jazz up a plain lampshade by gluing ribbon or ric rac braid around the edge.

8   Personalize white crockery with ceramic paints.

9   Give new life to a drab plastic or timber chair by decorating it with cut-out paper (maps, sheet music, magazine pages, wrapping paper, etc.) and sealing with a layer or two of clear varnish.

10 Cut any pretty leftover fabrics into squares for patchwork or triangles for bunting.

SELLING, GIVING AND RECYCLING

In the context of a Vintage/Modern home, being choosy is a good thing.

When a piece doesn't work in a scheme, and you're absolutely convinced that you can't transform it into something more useful or more beautiful, then you're better off simply getting rid of it, rather than living with it and hating it. Nurture a touch of ruthlessness: it will stand you in good stead.

But just how do you get rid of stuff? It's not always as easy as it sounds. The best option, obviously, is to sell it for as much money as possible, perhaps to a specialist dealer or second-hand shop, via an auction house, online or through the small ads. Bearing in mind that dealers will usually pay you only about half of what they expect to sell a piece for, and that auctions are, by their very nature, uncertain environments, you may feel that selling it yourself is the

ideal option. The pitfall here is that you have to do all the legwork, and may not manage to reach the right audience. Your eventual choice of method should, therefore, depend on what you're selling, its value and how much time and effort you want to put in.

Alternatively, you could try swapping an unwanted piece with friends or family, or by using an online swap community. If all else fails, you may end up giving it away. Again, try friends and relatives; otherwise, take it to your local furniture reuse centre or charity shop, or offer it on Freecycle or a similar online network. And bask in the knowledge that your discarded item will become a much-loved part of someone else's home.

Try swapping with friends, whether it's plants from your garden, unwanted furniture, a spot of DIY or an evening's babysitting.

ESSENTIALS

ARCHITECTURE

To create a truly successful Vintage/Modern scheme, it's essential to consider the architecture of your home.

It may be that your home's period style is so striking that you have no choice but to coordinate with it, or else consciously to clash or contrast. Lucky you – go for it! Make the most of cornices, ceiling roses, skirtings, door plates, key escutcheons and so on, in all their twiddly, twirly, old-fashioned glory. Or it may be that you have the blank canvas of a modern home, providing the ideal background for interesting furnishings and accessories.

In real life, though, most of us have houses with a few attractive details, but not enough to be properly cohesive. If that is the case, it's a good idea to work out what architectural look you're going for, then add whatever is necessary – modern versions, salvaged originals or bespoke reproductions – and perhaps even remove any details that detract from your desired style. It's amazing how much difference it can make to coordinate skirting boards, door surrounds and picture rails: they provide a room with subtle structure that you may not particularly notice, but would really miss if it wasn't there. You can make a major impact with even minor details, such as door handles and window catches, which should match stylistically and be made of the same material (mixing brass with chrome, for example, in a single room just looks weird). Removing naff or unwanted architectural details is, of course, a personal decision, but do exercise caution, particularly if you have the slightest suspicion that you're about to rip out anything original. If you really can't stand it, simply 'painting out' an unwanted feature is often as effective as a more drastic step.

Right: Plain, linear furnishings complement the simplicity of this contemporary room.

Above: Modern furniture blends seamlessly with the period details of this airy open-plan room.

Left: With such dramatic architecture as this, there's no need for elaborate furniture and accessories.

Opposite: Minimalist architecture makes a wonderful backdrop for the elaborate designs of antique furniture.

FURNITURE

Get creative with furniture and transform old, damaged or dull pieces into sassy, stylish pieces that will truly enhance your home.

Wardrobes and chests of drawers

The flat panels on large wardrobes or chests of drawers are crying out to be jazzed up with carefully cut wallpaper. Paint the remaining areas in a coordinating colour, and finish the whole with a coat of matt varnish. Sheet mirror on wardrobe doors is another idea, and useful, too, while a simple change of knobs makes a massive difference to the overall look.

Dining tables Sand back

and revarnish a stained tabletop, or, if that's not possible, paint over it. Alternatively, hide it entirely by covering with an antique damask or embroidered tablecloth or, for a very different look, a length of cheery oilcloth. For an everyday tablecloth, there's nothing wrong with a flat sheet.

Dressers Make your own simple dresser by hanging

a set of shelves above a chest of drawers, sideboard or cupboard. Either use matching timber or paint everything the same colour. A dull modern dresser can be transformed by adding decorative mouldings, or by pasting chintzy wallpaper behind the shelves.

Beds

Make a new headboard by stapling wadding around a rectangle of MDF and covering with a tactile fabric. If you have the DIY skills (or don't mind paying someone to do it for you), make it extra-tall, deeply buttoned and with wings – cosy and protective as well as ultra stylish. For an impromptu headboard, wallpaper an appropriately sized rectangle above the bed, prop up a folding screen, or hang a length of hemmed fabric from a batten.

Coffee tables and side tables

Paint and woodstain are quick and easy options. Alternatively, give an old table a funky new look by decorating the top with mosaic or découpage. If necessary, have a piece of glass cut to protect the new surface.

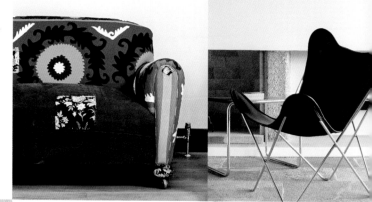

Dining chairs

These don't have to match but should have some similarity of shape, size or material. If they really conflict, paint them, or make simple loose covers as a disguise.

Sofas and armchairs

A comfortable and good-quality piece of upholstered furniture is worth its weight in gold, and can be wonderfully revived with a new cover. You can even alter the character and proportions of a piece by varying such details as piping, buttoning, pleating, ruffles and valances.

Right: These two delightful pieces of furniture are from different periods and in different styles, but, as well as the colour of the timber, their shapes echo each other nicely.

FABRIC

Fabric can be chic or kitsch,
spartan or sumptuous, practical
or inspirational, but whatever
its style, it is a key element of
a Vintage/Modern home.

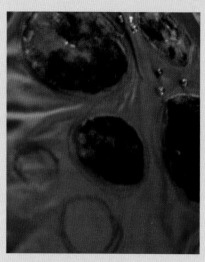

Key questions to ask when choosing fabric

- How wide is the fabric? Wider rolls of fabric are better value, and require less sewing.

- How heavy is it? Heavy fabrics may be too bulky for small projects, while light fabrics are likely to show wear more quickly.

- How durable is it? Fabric is divided into categories according to whether it can stand up to light, general or heavy domestic use.

- Is it washable? And, if so, is it pre-shrunk?

- If it's patterned, what size is the repeat? With large patterns you'll need to buy more fabric so that you can match the repeats.

By using fabric cleverly you can make a big design statement, unify a room or add delightful colour, pattern and texture. And, while it's alarmingly easy to blow the budget on luxury fabric, it's also possible, with a little ingenuity, to create an eye-catching look on a shoestring.

The days of fussy curtains are, thank goodness, long gone, and simple gathered curtains and Roman or roller blinds not only look lovely but also are easy and inexpensive to make yourself. To save on the cost of fabric, think laterally: sheets, tablecloths, an old pair of larger curtains, blankets, quilts, saris and lace panels are all options instead of conventional cut fabric, as long as the weight

Previous pages: Use fabric to add sumptuous texture, rich colour and delightful pattern to a room.

Above, left: Cushion covers with bold patterns will liven up any room. As here, they can be made very simply, with no fuss or frills.

Above, right: A gorgeous cacophony of different fabrics, united by their bold reds, looks fabulous in this kitsch kitchen.

Opposite: Whether woven or printed, plain or embellished, even small pieces of fabric can be cleverly employed for maximum effect.

and bulk of the fabric are suitable for the size of the window. Lengths of inexpensive plain fabric can be 'poshed up' with a contrasting border or interesting trim.

If you're fairly handy with a sewing machine, making a loose cover for a sofa or chair shouldn't be too daunting. Dispense with fancy piping and avoid using boldly striped fabric, which will show up any wobbly seams; when it comes to the fastenings, you could always cheat and use simple ties instead of zips, or even hook-and-loop tape.

For a fashionable patchwork look, use lengths of different (but coordinating) fabric; the same goes if you're making a duvet cover, bedspread or tablecloth. Or, if your sofa fabric is plain and uninteresting, simply pile pretty cushions on top. In fact, sumptuous effects can easily be created by employing expensive fabric in small quantities: as cushion fronts, covers for dining-chair seats, pillowcases, and so on. Fabrics are practical, versatile and, above all, inspirational, so experiment and have some fun.

LIGHTING

The best lighting is often invisible:
you don't notice the fitting itself,
but simply the fact that it illuminates
efficiently and beautifully, creating
a comfortable ambience and
contributing to an individual look.

Right: Concealed, ambient lighting creates soft, general illumination in this bedroom.

Below, right: Poul Henningsen's Artichoke lamp of 1958 is a classic that looks superb over a modern dining table.

Cleverly used, lighting can emphasize good points or disguise problem areas. It can also highlight colour, texture and form, and divide, unify or open up a space.

Experts work by layering different types of light: overall background light; bright lights for working by; accents of light for special features; and atmospheric lights for mellow pools of moodiness. But let's not get too hung up on technicalities. It's not difficult to work out that you need to have a bright light above your chopping board and be able to lower the lighting for a romantic supper. If possible, design a lighting scheme at the building-work stage, choosing from ceiling downlights, pendants or tracks, floor-level or wall-mounted uplighters, wall washers, floor lamps, table lamps and special display lighting. Or, for a quick upgrade on a budget (and let's face it, this is usually more realistic), you can get away with replacing main light switches with dimmers, and plugging in a selection of lamps around the room at strategic points and various heights.

That brings us to the other part lighting plays in a Vintage/ Modern scheme: through fittings – old or new – that add character and flair. They're accessories with distinctive colours, shapes and styles, and are as crucial to a room as are furniture and fabric, walls and window treatments. If you want your lighting to be anonymous, there are plenty of simple styles that will fit the bill, from wooden table lamps with coolie shades to the ubiquitous (and inexpensive) paper globe-shaped pendants. But if you'd rather integrate your lighting into a mix-and-match scheme, all sorts of fabulous and funky options will work, from an antique glass chandelier or a French rise-and-fall pendant to a Moroccan-style lantern, and from a green-shaded desk lamp to a glamorous, coloured-glass table lamp. Style, colour, material, size and shape will all influence how each fitting works with other furnishings, whether complementing or contrasting. And, last but definitely not least, consider how you could introduce a light-fitting that's a focal point in itself: perhaps a dramatic floor lamp, a striking contemporary chandelier or a groovy 1960s lava lamp.

Below, left: The Art Deco style of this wall lamp perfectly suits the acid green of the brickwork tiling.

Below: A twinkly glass chandelier looks gorgeous in a glamorous bedroom.

Opposite: A striking low-level lamp – especially one that can be dimmed to a pleasant glow when necessary – is always an asset in a dining room.

Light-fittings for a Vintage/Modern scheme

- Paper globes: cheap, timeless and attractive anywhere in the home.

- The classic Anglepoise lamp: dates back to the 1930s but is just as fabulous today; now available in a range of gorgeous colours.

- A pretty antique glass chandelier with clear or coloured drops: particularly lovely in a bedroom.

- An elegant, over-arching floor lamp: the Achille Castiglioni Arco lamp (see page 70) is the epitome, but you'll find some good imitations and variations.

- Fairy lights: string over mantelpieces, along shelves or across walls for a truly girly effect.

- A row of industrial-style aluminium pendant lights: perfect over a dining table or kitchen island.

- Cheap wooden lamp bases, in any shape or size: paint to suit you and add a home-made, vintage or contemporary shade.

WINDOW TREATMENTS

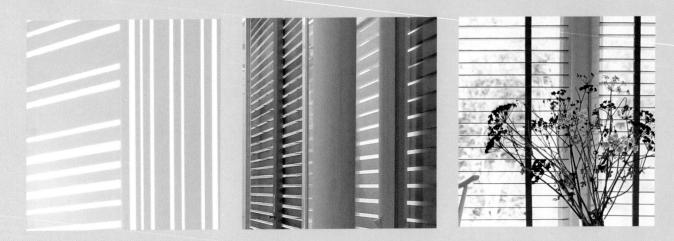

For warmth, cosiness and privacy, window treatments are a practical necessity. But much more than that, they add colour, pattern, texture and – if you want them to – eye-catching style to a room. Whatever you choose, well-designed curtains, blinds or shutters are crucial elements of a Vintage/Modern scheme.

Opposite: Roller blinds are inexpensive, unfussy and very practical, especially in a kitchen. They can also add a welcome jolt of colour and pattern.

Curtains

It's hard to beat the satisfyingly well-decorated feel that a pair of attractive curtains gives to a room. Indeed, they can be the making of a Vintage/Modern scheme. For subtle, minimal effect, choose a plain, neutral fabric and hang it in simple gathers; linen looks gorgeous, and antique linen sheets (picked up at auction or from a second-hand shop) can be headed, hemmed and hung with no great difficulty. Alternatively, use a patterned fabric that complements your scheme. If you fancy an informal look, don't use traditional, pleated or gathered header tape, but buy (or make) curtains with tab- or tie-tops, large eyelet holes, clips, hooks or a deep hem that slides over a pole.

Blinds

Blinds have a clean-lined look that's both sophisticated and laid-back – and the really good news is that they can be very cheap, requiring far less fabric than a full set of curtains, and are easy to make yourself. A roller blind in a neutral colour blends into the background of any scheme, while Roman blinds pull up in lovely soft folds for a chic effect. To pretty-up either, you could add a contrasting border and a good-looking pull, or even an amusing twist with a trim made from ribbon, ric rac, pompoms, stitching, fringing, shells or buttons.

Shutters

Shutters are my personal favourite: good-looking in an unfussy way, they're great for privacy, blocking out sound and light, and adding an extra layer of security. Shaker-style shutters have a timber frame and solid centre panel, can be left plain or painted any colour you like, and are ideal for a Georgian or Victorian home. American shutters, with tilting louvres for letting in the light, look fantastic and work virtually anywhere, while funky acrylic shutters – available in an array of colours – look stunning in a contemporary scheme or as a dramatic contrast to period details.

FLOORING

As the largest visible surface in any room, flooring is essential in setting the look and feel. A highly decorative floor will be a feature in its own right, and may require relatively plain furnishings, while a neutral floor can provide a sophisticated backdrop for an eclectic scheme.

The lowdown on rugs

The backbone of many a Vintage/Modern look, rugs come in many guises, and choosing one comes down to a combination of variables:

Pattern

It's generally a good idea to suit the type of pattern (modern, traditional, Oriental, etc.) to the overall style of the room. When it's an eclectic mix, choose a rug that doesn't overwhelm the other elements.

Size

It's important that the rug fits the space, neither overwhelming it nor looking like a pinprick in the middle of a large floor area. A rug that is slightly too large can be tucked under furniture. It's possible, although costly, to have a new rug made to a specific size.

Texture

The lovely texture a rug adds to a room is often its biggest benefit. Very shaggy rugs look glamorous but can be hard to keep smart; flat-woven rugs are more practical. Some pile rugs come in a mixture of heights to create interesting textural effects.

Colour

Choose a rug to complement other colours in the room, but also bear in mind that pale colours increase the sense of space, while dark colours are more cosy and attract the eye. Neutral colours are ideal for busy rooms.

Material

Wool is natural and durable, doesn't fade and is resistant to water, fire and stains (although a spilled glass of red wine will still cause a problem). Unfortunately, it's also more expensive than the artificial options. Synthetics can have a shiny look (although that may work in some settings), and are less likely than natural fibres to age well.

If you already have beautiful floors, congratulations! If not, there's no getting away from the fact that a new floor, whether wood or carpet, natural fibre, vinyl, linoleum, cork, rubber, stone or tile, is going to be fairly expensive. That said, there are clever ways to cheat on costs without cutting down on style. If you have timber floorboards (often hidden beneath grotty carpets), the most obvious solution is simply to renovate and paint them, or sand and re-stain them. There are plenty of pretty floor-paint colours, while a painted pattern of stripes or checks (mark it out with masking tape before you start) can be enormously attractive. In a utilitarian area, a concrete floor can be painted and sealed to surprisingly smart effect. And, if your carpets are less than pristine, it's worth hiring an industrial cleaner to sort them out. Rugs can hide a myriad of sins as well as pulling a Vintage/Modern look together. Although some can cost the earth, rugs needn't be expensive: most household auctions, for example, include piles of old rugs that will clean up a treat.

If you absolutely must replace your flooring, plain carpet is probably the cheapest option (I like to pay a little extra for natural wool), and the better wood laminates can be lovely. Both go beautifully with all sorts of decor. If you're lucky, you might find some 'pre-loved' timber boards at a salvage yard; other places to try for cheap flooring include discount outlets, factory shops and, of course, the good old sales.

Previous page: Natural floor coverings now come in a huge range of colours and styles, from the rustic to the dashingly smart.

Above, left: The warmth and patina of old timber floorboards are particularly wonderful in a bedroom.

Left: The soft luxury of a sheepskin rug provides a stunning textural contrast to the shiny stone floor beneath.

WALLCOVERINGS

While painted walls are undoubtedly quick, cheap and easy, sometimes only a more elaborate treatment will do justice to your Vintage/ Modern scheme.

So fashionable – and so much fun – wallpaper creates a fabulously individual effect, whether in a boldly coloured, modern, abstract design or a pretty, chintzy, traditional style. It's important to pick a pattern that suits the size of the room, unless you're going for drama by using an oversized pattern in a small space. If you're worried that it will become overwhelming, cover just one wall (that saves money, too). Remember that very small patterns disappear at a distance, leaving you with the effect of a plain colour. For an unusual and striking look, paper a room with one pattern but use a different colourway for one or two drops. Textured wallpapers add a lovely tactile element, but sheeny-shiny metallic papers – super-sophisticated and great for reflecting light – are best used only where the wall beneath is very smooth and flat.

Contemporary wallpapers can be highly graphic, hand-finished with cut-work, stitching or appliqué, interactive (colour-your-own or add stickers), three-dimensional (incorporating crystals, beading, sequins or even tiny LEDs) or digitally printed to your own design, perhaps using colours to match your room. And, of course, these days bathrooms and kitchens can be either papered with a moisture-resistant product or given a protective coating; alternatively, use wallpaper as a splashback, with a rectangle of glass or acrylic fixed over the top.

Above, left: Toile de Jouy wallpaper is more often seen in a traditional setting, but this quirky use on a sloping ceiling is pretty and appealing.

Left and opposite: Strong prints are bold and dynamic, and can be the focal point of a room. Sometimes they're best limited to just one wall, however, or even a single panel.

More ways to decorate your walls

- Huge digital images can be pasted over an entire wall.

- Wall stickers come in all sorts of divine designs and are removable if you feel like a change.

- Magnetic wallpaper or paint allows you to stick anything you like – pictures, homework, notes, etc. – to the wall with magnets.

- Blackboard paint is ideal for a wall in a child's room or a home office.

- Large maps (old or new) are both attractive and educational.

- Offcuts of vintage wallpaper, or by the same token any smallish papers, such as sheet music or wrapping paper, can be either collaged straight on to the wall, or framed as individual works of art.

- Posters don't look impressive if they're just taped to the walls, but frame them nicely and hang in an orderly way and the result is much more grown-up.

- Fabric hangings – whether a length of embroidery or appliqué, an old patchwork quilt, a dhurrie or kilim, blanket or sari – add warmth and character.

ACCESSORIES

Just as a nondescript dress can be transformed with the addition of a fabulous belt and handbag, so the very plainest of rooms can be made sumptuous and stunning with clever accessorizing. And, for a Vintage/ Modern beginner, this is also a great way to experiment without mistakes being too costly or time-consuming.

You could start by sorting out your cushions: perhaps make a matching set in this season's colour or most fashionable pattern, or gather a glorious jumble, old or new, in delicious prints and plains. Make cushions from remnants, or buy small lengths of luxury fabric; it won't cost the earth and it can really transform a dull sofa.

Then turn your attention to the walls. A brilliant way to make a statement is with an oversized antique or retro mirror (you can still pick them up relatively cheaply), or even a series of them, grouped together. Pictures or prints always look better in coordinating frames. And don't hang them randomly; align them vertically or horizontally, or, if they're in a group, lay them out on the floor first and stand on a chair to get an idea of how they'll work together.

Above, right: Just one splendid cushion, such as this scarlet example with relief trimming, can make a room.

Right: This display of carefully chosen ceramics, with intense colours and interesting shapes, is inspired.

Ceramics and glassware, whether practical or purely decorative, can add either pretty pattern or strong shapes and bold colours, depending on the style you choose. You can easily mix old and new if you choose a theme and stick to it – chintzy pottery or bright glass vases, for example. Car boot sales, general auctions and junk shops can all yield bargains, and my best advice is to be selective: choose only the most special pieces, then arrange with a sense of order, whether you aim for formal symmetry, align them in neat rows or group by colour, shape or height. A thoughtful display will make the cheapest of accessories look enviably classy and chic.

Above: Their lustrous surfaces and neutral colours make this arrangement of small, pretty accessories cohere particularly well.

Left: Black-and-white family photographs create an enchanting display.

TECHNOLOGY

With a few honourable exceptions (we'll get to those later), modern technology doesn't particularly suit a Vintage/Modern scheme. In an ideal world, you'd have a separate home office and a multimedia/screening room, with your music piped invisibly through the house … but for those of us on planet Earth, here are some less expensive ideas for dealing with intrusive technology.

Simplest of all, wall-mount a TV on a swivelling arm so that it can be swung out of the way when not in use, perhaps into a corner, behind a curtain, screen or sliding door, or even into a purpose-built niche or cupboard. If you can't do that, at least avoid horrible purpose-built stands, and put the TV on top of an attractive sideboard, table or chest of drawers, or have a sturdy shelf built specially. Bulky music systems, and such computer peripherals as printers and scanners, can also be hidden in cupboards; if you have separate speakers, they can be tucked at the back of high shelves rather than stood on very visible wall brackets. And, when upgrading your computing gear, consider a laptop with wireless connectivity, which will get rid of trailing cables and give you the ultimate flexibility

Rather than hide it away, you can always show off your technology, whether it's a music system or a television, by investing in a cool, retro style and making it a feature of the room.

118

in your workspace. You could store the laptop in a drawer, keep the router on a kitchen dresser and hide the printer under the stairs, for example. Alternatively, consider investing in a purpose-made home office-in-a-cupboard – one that can be hidden away behind attractive doors that complement the rest of the room.

The opposite scenario is one in which you celebrate technology, showing it off in all its glory. You may, for example, find that a slim and sleek flat-screen TV actually enhances the room, or you could seek out a funky, retro-style example in a bold colour and interesting shape. Modern music players are often sculptural objects worth treating as an ornament, while more and more computer equipment now comes in pretty colours or even unusual cladding, such as textured leather. Now that's definitely better than a grey plastic box.

The slimmer and sleeker televisions become, the easier it is to tuck them away somewhere so that they're unobtrusive, but can still easily be used when required.

119

BATHROOMS

Unless you really want to flash the cash, we're not talking here about completely renovating your bathroom. Fortunately, opting for the Vintage/Modern look means you don't have to.

Instead, you can turn a bland or outdated bathroom into a stylistic haven with a few simple, quick and inexpensive changes that combine the appeal of the old with the functionality of the new.

The easiest alteration is to repaint or paper the walls for an instant and dramatic transformation. You may (although this isn't quite so straightforward) be able to clad the lower half of the walls in tongue-and-groove panelling, building a ledge along the top for toiletries and ornaments. This has the advantage of hiding ugly pipework, as well as adding a pleasantly retro-countrified feel to what can otherwise be a rather cold, anonymous space. Or it may be possible to add some beautiful tiles, either on a bare wall or over existing tilework. If you're covering only a small space, choose the most luxurious tiles you can afford for a truly sumptuous effect.

Above: This clever tongue-and-groove panelling incorporates shelving, drawers and a mirror. It's useful to sneak extra storage into a bathroom.

Left: A prettily papered wall and a lick of paint can quickly revitalize a tired bathroom.

Above: An interesting display works well with the monochrome colour palette of this elegant bathroom.

Right: A modern hand-painted mural provides a pretty backdrop for a traditional roll-top bath.

How about changing the taps? Ugly, cheap ones can be replaced relatively easily with either minimalist modern or period-style examples – a vast improvement. Wall-hung mirrors, too, can easily be changed: instead of a conventional bathroom mirror, consider cool retro types, in unusual shapes and with interesting frames. Can you replace the flooring? New linoleum is lovely; wood laminate isn't terribly expensive; and a good vinyl in an attractive colour and pattern can make an enormous difference. If all else fails, throw down a pretty rug. And please don't put up with horrid old towels: either invest in a new set or dye your old ones a gorgeous colour; you could even stitch on narrow trims in coordinating vintage fabric.

Lastly, the all-important storage. A little pine cupboard or chest of drawers will easily conceal most of the kit you don't want to display, or you could opt for coloured plastic boxes, some simple lidded baskets or a row of handmade drawstring bags hung from hooks on the back of the door. Look for toothbrush holders, soap dishes, jars, pots and so on in pleasing shapes, colours and textures, perhaps smooth glass or stainless steel, turned wood, mosaic, bamboo, enamel, wirework, floral china or pressed glass – many of which can be picked up for a song in second-hand shops.

Above, right:
A salvaged washbasin can be the focal point of a bathroom, especially with a splashback made from interesting tiles.

Right: Free-standing bathroom furniture is often relatively inexpensive. United by a certain delicacy of form and a muted colour scheme, it looks stylish here.

KITCHENS

By applying the Vintage/Modern vibe, you can give a tired old kitchen a chic new look without breaking the bank.

Let's first tackle what can be the biggest bugbear: dated, dirty or just plain disgusting cupboards. Provided the basic structure is sound, you can stain or repaint the doors and drawer-fronts – and replace the knobs or handles while you're at it. If a paint job won't disguise the unattractive style of the doors, buy replacements: it's more costly, but still a whole lot cheaper than forking out for a new kitchen, and a great way to make a dramatic change to the look of the room. Or you could get rid of the fitted kitchen either partially or entirely, instead opting for a dresser, sideboards, chests of drawers, tables, shelves and racks; always remember to keep their depth roughly the same (so that some don't jut into the room more than others), and align your shelving to pull the room together visually.

Opposite: Strong colours can work extremely well in a kitchen, especially when the overall feeling is laid-back and simple.

Right: This free-standing unit is not only extremely useful but also attractive in itself.

Below, right: Run out of storage space? Simply add a rail and some butcher's hooks on which to hang pots, pans and utensils.

Replacing the worktops will update and upgrade your kitchen instantly, and the least expensive options are laminate (buy the best you can afford) and timber (don't put it next to a sink). Think about lighting, too. You could, for example, swap a boring ceiling spotlight track for a similar fitting that has a little more edge, fit a dimmer switch to the main light to give atmospheric options at different times of the day, and – if you have a dining area in the kitchen – hang a row of three or more identical pendant lights over the table. Last, but by no means least, get to work on coordinating your kitchen kit. A jumble of garishly coloured mugs and some petrol-station glasses won't cut the mustard, but hiding them in a cupboard and showing off just a few treasured finds, heirlooms or designer chef's accessories is a recipe for success.

CASE STUDIES

CASEY'S STORES
FOR BETTER VALUE

GIFTS

CHEAP AND CHIC

1

Proving that you don't have to be big to be beautiful, the bijou living space in this city-centre flat is furnished with second-hand finds that cost hardly anything but are pricelessly high on style.

Opposite: White-painted walls make the most of high ceilings, and light floods in through tall windows.

Above, left: Pattern is carefully restricted so as not to be overpowering. This has extended to upholstering only one of the two chairs in a pretty rose print.

Above, right: The deep red of the densely patterned rug provides the starting point for the colour scheme.

When it comes to decorating your home, a shortage of cash isn't necessarily a bad thing. It forces you to be inventive, and that, in turn, can result in unexpected solutions and exciting creativity. Take this city-centre flat, for example. Owned by a designer who specializes in quirky prints, flea-market style and nostalgia with a modern twist, it has barely a single new, shop-bought item in it. Instead, most of the furnishings are cherished hand-me-downs from family and friends, and kitsch accessories that are the product of years spent scouring car boot sales, junk shops and antiques centres.

High ceilings and large windows make the room intrinsically appealing, and the owner has made the most of them by painting the walls white and putting up ultra-simple canvas blinds that fold right up above the windows to allow in the maximum amount of light. Leaving such architectural features as banisters, skirting boards and the fire surround in their unpainted timber gives a sense of naturalness and warmth, as well as providing a simple unity. I love the inspirational wall of postcards, sketches and pictures torn from magazines, and the fact that open shelving (always the cheapest storage option) has been used to create casual displays – whether of haphazardly stacked books, CDs or a treasured red-and-white tea set.

It's not a huge room, but every inch of space has been used to its best advantage, from the shelved alcoves either side of the fireplace to the cupboard between the windows and the utilitarian shelving under the stairs. Even the small fold-out table has hampers piled below it, and the coffee table has a handy shelf for stacks of magazines.

These 1950s chairs, one upholstered in a stylized rose print that's typical of the decade, are both practical and attractive.

Strong red is the predominant colour in the scheme, and this neatly arranged retro crockery makes a lovely display.

Overall, though, it's colour and pattern that are fundamental to the success of this room. Colour is largely restricted to the natural tones of timber and leather, with grey, a strong red – which predominates – and a touch of sky blue. Pattern is limited, too, to the dense geometric floral of the large rug, a more blowsy floral on the smaller rug, and a typically 1950s print on one of the armchairs. Anything more and – since the room is crammed with mismatching furniture and accessories – it could easily become fussy and confusing. There's also the subject of style. Here, it is predominantly the low, lean look of the 1950s: chairs with slim upholstery, a coffee table with splayed legs, and an ultra-utilitarian folding table are key pieces, while others, such as the Lloyd Loom chair and battered chesterfield sofa, are so timelessly traditional that, given a little care (one painted white, the other given coordinating cushions), they'll go with anything. This combination of inexpensive, informal pieces is very successful, and the overall result is relaxed and comfortable, unpretentious and very good-looking.

Above, left: An open area under the stairs is the ideal place for a set of shelves. Here, they're used to display cherished collections of retro items.

Left: A random collection of images creates an inspiring display and can be changed as often as you like.

2

CLASSIC ELEGANCE

Striking period details make this an
amazing flat in itself. Furnished with a
sophisticated mix of old and new pieces,
it has unique, timeless appeal.

KEY FEATURES

Hanging a bold modern painting over a classic fireplace produces a dramatic clash of styles that really works.

These cushions provide almost the only splash of pattern in the room. They're decorative without being over the top.

Blessed with floor-to-ceiling windows that flood the room with light and lead to a gorgeous outdoor terrace, this London flat has a head start in the feel-good stakes. But it's the architectural details – high walls, relief plasterwork, panelled shutters and an imposing fireplace – that make it truly outstanding. The trick for the owner, a dealer in French antiques, was to complement those features without clashing with them, and she has pulled it off with aplomb.

The combination of furniture is unexpected. Rather than the expensive, coordinating antiques one might have anticipated, the owner has chosen a traditional rug, a squashy modern sofa, a scrolled metal-and-glass coffee table and a pair of mismatching old armchairs, one in leather, the other wicker. But each carefully chosen piece is strong yet simple in shape and, arranged almost symmetrically, they become timeless and relate perfectly to one another. Even the table lamps in each corner are completely different, yet match almost exactly in shape and size. This is all the more effective because there's no clutter: the walls are white, the floor is plain and pale, the windows

are bare, and pattern is restricted to the paintings on the walls (again, symmetrically arranged for unity, and with complementary frames), the books and a matching set of understated sofa cushions. It's a great look to emulate, wherever your furnishings originate: keep things simple and to a minimum, then arrange everything formally, and you won't go far wrong.

Thanks to the muted colour scheme in the main part of the living room, it's the colourful painting over the fireplace that draws the eye. Around the corner, however, the owner has allowed herself the indulgence of a chaise longue covered in purple velvet, while the luxe feel is continued with an elegant mirrored sideboard. Here, in a hidden corner, full-height built-in shelving houses hundreds of books and carefully arranged displays – family photos, china, much-loved collections – easily to hand but not in full view all the time.

This mix of antique, vintage and modern shows panache and an eye for quality in whatever form it may come. Cool, calm and carefully composed, yet comfortable and relaxed, this is classic luxury with a subtle and appealing twist.

Page 133: An eclectic mix of furnishings, formally arranged, complements the striking architecture of this gracious flat.

Opposite: Although made of completely different materials, in form and colour these chairs almost appear to be a matching pair.

Right: Luscious velvet upholstery gives this antique chaise longue a modern look.

MODERN RETRO

In a nineteenth-century former mission hall, modern architecture contrasts with warm wood and a fabulous collection of vintage furnishings.

3

The conversion of a church frequently creates wonderfully huge, open spaces, and this 'tin tabernacle' of 1895 was no exception. The living area is large and open, and an ultra-modern floating mezzanine has been inserted above to make the most of the space, creating two double bedrooms inside the soaring roof. The daring contrast of this brand new glass, steel and white-painted-concrete structure with the knotty wood-panelled walls and darkly glossy timber floor is delicious and, perhaps surprisingly, works a treat.

So, just how do you furnish a living space like this? Well, the owners are – to put it mildly – crazy about vintage, which made 1950s and 1950s-style furniture an obvious choice. But this is no museum-like re-creation of the era. As well as a classic sideboard/chest of drawers and some swish black-leather upholstery, they've chosen cosy velour and a mad shaggy rug, with highlights of bold printed florals, faux leopard skin and colourful crochet. The icing on the cake is a collection of kitsch prints; let's just say that poodles are a predominant feature.

And the reason it all works is that, in what is actually a rather pared-down setting, the furniture is clean-lined and simple in outline, with typically 1950s spindly, splayed legs and similarly toned solid blocks of dark colour. The room has a thoughtful unity. Even the modern, free-standing stove has sympathetically simple features, as do the old cinema seats and the antique wooden divan, which together form a cosy secondary seating area, illuminated by a low-hung retro glass pendant. Accessories aren't overdone, and the pictures, with coordinating frames, are grouped evenly and neatly. This eclectic but functional and comfortable living space didn't cost an arm and a leg to put together, and is not just friendly and welcoming, but also interesting, quirky and fun.

Opposite: A modern mezzanine floats above the living area and contrasts dramatically with the timber-clad walls of the former mission hall.

Below: Retro style can also be incredibly comfortable.

Bottom: You can pick up prints for a song at car boot sales; but you must frame and hang them well in order to add style as well as kitsch humour.

KEY FEATURES

The gorgeous velvet-upholstered swivel seat, based on Arne Jacobsen's 'Egg' chair of 1958, really sets the retro tone.

You can't beat a wood-burner for creating a feeling of warmth and comfort. Even modern examples, such as this, have a timeless style.

TIMELESS CHARM

Classic architecture is combined with an
eclectic selection of furniture and quirky
touches in this delightful family home.

4

5

ALL WHITE NOW

By opening up a dingy front room, the owner of this Victorian house has created a gorgeously light and airy living space that comfortably mixes pieces from different periods – as long as they're white.

When a room is small, dark and unattractive, there's only one thing to be done: a radical alteration that takes it from run-down to rather splendid. This delightful living room was once utterly unappealing, but has been transformed from ugly duckling to elegant swan and is now a smart and sassy single girl's pad.

This Victorian terraced house badly needed more space and light, and it doesn't take much to see that removing the wall to a gloomy, narrow front hall has made an enormous difference, allowing light to pour into the space. Inserting frosted glass panels into the traditional-style front door also helped, as did keeping the window treatments plain, pale and simple. The biggest trick, though, was to allow only one colour – white. White-painted floors, white fabric for the sofa, white chairs, a white desk, a white coffee table, white shelving, white lighting, white candles, even white flowers; it's hard to find much that isn't white anywhere in the room. The result is serene and peaceful, bright and airy, with an amazing feeling of spaciousness.

Another technique was to employ reflective surfaces as much as possible, to bounce light all around the room: hence the large mirror over the fireplace and the use of silver (from table legs to picture frames) and transparent acrylic. Texture, too, makes a difference. The floor isn't just white, it's glossy, reflective white, while the coffee table is similarly shiny, as is the wooden mirror frame. One cushion is all sparkly sequins, and even the chair upholstery and the mother-of-pearl light-fitting possess a certain shimmer.

But the ubiquitous use of white has another purpose, which is to pull together a nicely edited collection of furnishings from different eras and in different styles. A Louis-style chair, with pretty curved legs and carving, looks great next to a simple, modern sofa, a sleek, designery coffee table and a traditional desk. Nothing jars, and where there is a splash of colour, in the form of a Union Jack doormat and a few umbrellas in a stand, it produces a pleasing contrast without disturbing the room's coherence.

There's nothing particularly expensive here, yet the space has a sophisticated edge that contradicts its minimal budget. It just goes to show that, with the willingness to undergo a small amount of structural work, and the discipline to stick to a tightly focused scheme, it's possible to create a truly beautiful Vintage/Modern look that is also incredibly liveable.

Previous page: The demolition of a wall between the hall and the living room opened up the space. Light now floods through the room from the glazed front door and the large bay window.

Below, left: A mother-of-pearl pendant light has just the right shimmer and delicacy – and, of course, it has to be white.

Below, right: Modern furniture combines slender shapes and slim legs with reflective silver and gloss-white for maximum effect.

Sequins and a smooth, shiny upholstery fabric give this Louis-style chair reflective qualities.

Mirrors help to reflect light around a room; this one is a particularly pretty example.

French period style and a plain modern sofa are brought together by their colour and similarly curvy shapes.

URBAN REALISM

A 1970s renovation resulted in an open-plan flat that now combines raw, exposed beams and brickwork with classic designer furniture in strong, dark colours.

6

Opposite: Monumental furnishings and dark, moody colours suit the flat's architectural style.

Left: Brown is the unifying colour, while all the furniture, although large, is plain and simple in outline.

Below: Open metal shelves complement the brick walls, and provide masses of storage and an excellent display area.

KEY FEATURES

Exposed brick walls set the gritty tone of this city-centre flat.

A pair of kitsch, decorative lamps is in complete contrast to the industrial aesthetic of the room.

It may look like an industrial loft space, but in fact this dramatic, open-plan flat is on the top floor of a Georgian terraced house. The architecture is very important here: an exposed brick wall sets the gritty tone, as do the wooden beams running across the ceiling, complemented by unadorned, wood-framed sash windows and rough, sanded floorboards. These raw materials create fabulously interesting, uncompromising textures, raw and hard-edged. Entirely urban and unpretentious, the space offers very little in the way of frills or flounces.

Correspondingly, the furnishings for this open-plan living/dining/kitchen space were chosen for their simple, monumental shapes, dark and moody colours, and – with some notable exceptions – industrial aesthetic. Although perfectly comfortable and functional, the point is that they're big and tough-looking, not for wimps: take the huge modular sofa, arching designer lamp, leather chairs, tall steel shelving (ideal for storing loads of stuff in a space that has no built-

in cupboards) and factory-style, black-metal pendant lamps, for example. In minimal frames, the contemporary art on the walls is similarly dramatic and graphic. Into this mix, however, have been thrown some interesting oddities. A medieval bench seat, a wicker-seated rocking chair and rustic, panelled kitchen cupboards are just three. No doubt they were picked up for a song in second-hand shops or antiques outlets, yet they blend well because they have the same oversized, understated look as the rest of the furnishings. An animal-print rug offers a little pattern diversion, and then, just for a laugh, a pair of fabulously kitsch table lamps has been added, with prancing-stallion bases and acid-yellow shades. They're the absolute antidote to the pared-down toughness of the other pieces, yet that's precisely why they're there. Nothing in this home is conventional, and the lamps prove the point very happily.

EASY LIVING

A casual mix of old, new and retro makes
this kitchen/living room/diner a laid-
back, comfortable and informal space
in which to kick back and relax.

7

When you have a young family, an all-in-one
space in which you can cook, supervise
homework and then all collapse on the sofa is
absolutely ideal. The trick is to make this a space
that performs all those functions efficiently without
losing its sense of style. Here, it's the epitome of
family comfort, yet also effortlessly good-looking
in an easy-going, unpretentious way.

What's immediately apparent is that there
are very few new pieces in this relaxed open-
plan space. Instead, vintage and junk-shop
finds mingle with gifts, hand-me-downs and
the occasional piece of art. The main pieces of
furniture – a sofa, armchairs, a coffee table and
a dining table – are all as old as the hills, with
scuffs, chips and saggy bits to prove it. But don't
they look great? They've been jazzed up with
throws, blankets, cushions and, in the case of the
second-hand dining table, a coat of grey paint,
and all look as comfy as anything, with a certain
down-to-earth, beaten-up charm that really suits
the room's architecture, with its huge granite
fireplace and lofty, beamed ceiling. The dining
chairs are a mixed-up lot, some painted, some
left as they are, but they're absolutely in keeping
with the overall feel. Meanwhile, the kitchen is
almost as unlike a kitchen as it's possible to be,
with open-fronted units that look like bookcases,
and solid-wood worktops that blend with the bare
timber used elsewhere.

Opposite: Lit by skylights, the space has an informal, comfortable feel that's very welcoming.

Right: At the far end of the room, a selection of battered old chairs is grouped around a large stone fireplace.

LOVE

Painting chairs is a great way to disguise flaws, unify different styles and create a pretty effect overall.

Small kitchen accessories, such as these pressed-glass bowls, make a beautiful display.

In common with many open-plan spaces, this one is long and thin, and so has been divided into separate areas, for lounging, eating and cooking. The back of the sofa and a large rug provide one informal partition, while the L-shaped kitchen units add another; each area works for its own purpose, but it's also possible to see the room in its entirety, enjoying the sense of space and light. The owner's choice of artificial lighting – a chandelier above the cosy sitting area, a witch's ball over the dining table and ship's lanterns in the kitchen – has also helped to differentiate the spaces. Works of art and attractive accessories, from graphic prints to jugs of flowers picked from the garden, are dotted about. With a neutral background palette of grey and brown, these add flashes of colour: chalky pink, turquoise and the odd dash of cerise. It's the sort of place where you can put your feet up and relax without worrying about rucking up the sofa cover or putting down your mug of tea – in fact, an ideal family living space.

Above, left: The unpretentious dining table, with its delightful carved legs, has been painted an attractive mid-grey.

Above, right: The colours of a vintage poster pick up those of the glassware displayed beneath.

The simplest designs are always the best: it's when you start to complicate things that they can go wrong. Here, everything is in its rightful place; it's supremely comfortable, highly practical and (it goes without saying) very attractive.

The long, thin room is the ground floor of a traditional terraced house, and would once have been a warren of small, dark spaces. Now opened up so that you walk into the living area, through to the dining room, then into the kitchen and to the back door beyond, it's lit from two sides and offers plenty of space in which to spread out and relax. Golden floorboards stretch from front to back, window treatments are minimal, and walls are white for optimum neutrality. This is a palette against which anything can be put.

When you can see your kitchen from your sofa, it's essential that it fits the living-room vibe, and also that it can be kept tidy without too much effort. This one is pretty in a minimal kind of way, with plain white doors and drawer-fronts and a luxurious marble worktop. A slender, painted-wood shelf rather than a row of wall cupboards ensures that it doesn't feel cramped or overly utilitarian. Tidiness is made easier by the incredibly useful walk-in pantry at the back, and by the presence of so much hidden storage. That said, everything that needs to be at hand – knives, pans, coffee machine, breadboard – is within easy reach.

What's so effective about this space, I think, is the understated nature of everything in it. The pieces, old, new and eclectic though they are – from roughly planked dining table to soft, squashy sofa, and from shiny metal range cooker to ornate mirrored wardrobe – are unified by their simple shapes and unpretentious good looks. There's an appreciation of quality and a relaxed confidence that are supremely appealing.

Opposite: This front-to-back open-plan room offers plenty of light and space, and makes it easy for the cook to socialize at the same time.

Above, left: An abundance of natural light makes this a really pleasant room.

Above, right: Open-plan spaces need to be carefully planned. Here, coat hooks are tucked behind the front door, while an ornate mirrored wardrobe provides handy extra storage.

Right: The decorative looks of this rather grand range cooker make it an attractive part of the living space, rather than just another useful but dull piece of kitchen equipment.

Below: The pale veining of this marble worktop and splashback contributes an air of luxury. Open storage looks lovely, provided it can be kept tidy.

KEY FEATURES

This planked dining table is relaxed and comfortable, and looks great with more ornate pieces.

A traditional candelabra adds not just prettiness but also a witty contrast when placed on the rough-and-ready wooden table.

10

SIMPLE UTILITY

On the upper floor of a seaside cottage, simple, functional furnishings have been put together as inexpensively as possible to create a cosy space for cooking, eating and living.

A utility-style cabinet makes an ideal kitchen cupboard. You can pick up something similar in virtually any second-hand shop, and paint it.

The classic Anglepoise lamp looks great in all situations and is ideally suited to the aesthetic of this space.

This 1930s seaside cottage tucked behind a high-street shop has been dragged into the twenty-first century on a tiny budget, and is now fitted with electricity and heated by a wood-burning stove. The first floor is one huge space, with a kitchen at one end and an open-tread staircase leading to a sleeping platform at the other. Thanks to a combination of salvaged and second-hand pieces that date mostly from the 1930s, 1940s and 1950s, the look is both individual and welcoming, a sort of homely industrial chic.

The bones of the scheme are simple: a reclaimed wooden floor and walls that are plastered and painted white, left as bare brick or covered in plain white tiles. The space has been opened up to the roof, so the extra height makes for a feeling of even greater space. But it's the furnishings that make the room so appealing. For a start, there's the entirely unfitted kitchen, based on a huge wooden clothes chest that once graced a Parisian department store, its drawers perfect for

pots and pans. A cooker and a sink are tucked away to either side, and the fridge is housed beneath a length of timber that provides work-surface space. A utility-style cabinet makes a great larder, while wall-hung shelves are ideal for glasses, crockery, spices and so on. Anything extra can be popped into a basket, bucket or box. This is an object lesson in how to create a workable kitchen from practically nothing, at minimal cost.

The other furniture is equally down to earth, from the unassuming sofa to the planked wooden dining table with its range of mismatching chairs, and from the rustically hewn side table to the classic Anglepoise lamp. In terms of style, they're all simple pieces in muted, plain colours, made from inexpensive natural materials; there is nothing fussy, frilly or ostentatious. It just goes to show that the lack of a big budget can in fact be a catalyst to creativity, and is certainly no hindrance to creating a good-looking, comfortable and functional space.

Previous page: An open-tread staircase leading to a mezzanine sleeping platform bisects the room, separating the dining and living spaces.

Above: In the kitchen area the walls are tiled for practicality. Elsewhere they are bare or, where necessary, plastered and painted white, for a lovely, unpretentious contrast of textures.

Above: The gorgeous old chest of drawers was once in a French department store; now it's ideal for holding pots and pans.

Right: The satiny gloss of polished, reclaimed floorboards makes a perfect base for the room. Extra cosiness is provided by a selection of traditional rugs.

RETRO COLOUR

By keeping it simple and making the most of vintage finds, this sweet, colourful kitchen demonstrates great style on a limited budget.

A small kitchen in a city-centre flat may not seem the most inspiring of starting points. Yet with a clever combination of simple fittings, pretty colours and vintage accessories, the room manages to be both practical and inspirational.

The basics are a couple of white Shaker-style base units, with slim bar handles and a solid-wood worktop. Gathered curtains in a distinctively 1950s-style pattern soften the look (and are a cheaper option than solid doors to conceal the open-fronted cupboards), while a high shelf with a long rail beneath completes the practical storage. The cooker and fridge are free-standing, and extra bits and pieces can be stacked on the plate rack or popped into a white china jug. On the opposite wall, which is painted a pretty duck-egg blue, a set of shelves, with a few hooks screwed in, provides space for a display of gorgeous vintage crockery, patiently collected over the years, all prettily patterned and in delightful sorbet colours. A slender dining table and a couple of painted wooden chairs provide a place to sit comfortably while chatting to the cook, or for several people to enjoy an informal meal. This room combines function and aesthetic appeal with care and flair. As a recipe for making the most of a small space without spending a fortune, it really works.

Opposite: The ingredients of this kitchen are simple and minimal: a free-standing cooker, a couple of panelled cupboards, a shelf with a hanging rail and a plate rack. There is nothing costly or fancy, but such details as the pretty curtains and the coloured crockery make it look very appealing.

Above, left: Squeezing even a tiny table into a kitchen will always be incredibly useful.

Above, right: Screw a few hooks into a set of shelves to increase the available storage space as well as to add interest to the display.

KEY FEATURES

The use of gathered fabric (especially in a retro print) instead of doors lends a nostalgic and informal feel.

A set of shelves filled with pretty vintage crockery makes a delightful display, and keeps the china handy for everyday use.

FRENCH POLISH

12

An open, airy layout combined with classic French furnishings give this kitchen/diner laid-back elegance and timeless appeal.

KEY FEATURES

The classic black-and-white tiled floor unifies the room. Laid on the diagonal, it creates an illusion of extra space.

The turquoise of these antique French rise-and-fall lamps (ideal for providing soft light over a dining table) coordinates prettily with the painted, French-style cupboards.

Opposite:
Unpretentious school-style wooden chairs work perfectly with a simple wooden table, a foil for the more decorative French antiques in this part of the open-plan space.

Above, right: The kitchen side of the room is more workmanlike, with simple cupboards and chunky granite worktops. Instead of conventional wall-mounted units, a wooden shelf creates a fresh and open feel.

Tempting though it may be to stuff every inch of space in your kitchen with matching cupboards, it can be better to make the effort to come up with a more interesting solution. Of course, it helps if you're blessed with a relatively large area, but even in a small kitchen it's possible to replace a bland unit with one that has more character, or a wall cupboard with a simple shelf that you can use to display your more attractive kitchen kit.

In this gorgeous kitchen/diner, for example, there's not a wall unit in sight, and very little 'matches' in the conventional way, giving the room a relaxed, uncluttered feel. With base cupboards and an island unit in a mix of painted and natural wood, the owners have opted for shelves, racks and a pair of tall free-standing cupboards with masses of space for crockery and glassware (they're open-fronted, so tidiness is essential). These French-style cupboards, which face each other across the dining area, are the most decorative element of the room, coordinating

with the antique rise-and-fall lamps and a panelled overmantel mirror. The kitchen end is more functional, with the simple outlines of cupboards, shelves and work surfaces, inset ceramic sinks and stainless-steel appliances.

An important unifying factor is the charming black-and-white floor, which echoes the pale walls and chunky, matt granite worktops. It is tiled on the diagonal for interest and to create the illusion of more space; a similar effect could be achieved with linoleum or vinyl, or by carefully marking out and painting timber boards. Lastly, the accessories on show are by no means all in the same style or from the same era, but what they have in common, apart from a pleasingly limited colour palette of blues, greens and browns, is classic, enduring appeal: copper pans, Cornishware, earthenware crocks, Chinese porcelain. In keeping with the room as a whole, they have plenty of character but are eclectic in a way that's chic, discreet and unfussy.

PARED-DOWN AND PRACTICAL

13

A consistent palette of clean, simple lines
and limited, strong colours are the basics
for a functional but sophisticated kitchen.

Left: Keeping it simple,
the main elements of
the room are clean-
lined, pared-down and
in a minimal range of
strong colours.

Opposite, left: A walk-
in larder is every cook's
dream. Here, slim
shelves store stacks
of preserves and
dry goods.

Opposite, right: Open
storage and a station
clock are ideally suited
to the functional look
and feel of this room.

There's something of the professional kitchen about this room. Maybe it's the bistro-style crockery, or the brick-shaped white tiles, the oversized metal pendant lamps, or the everything-to-hand wooden shelving. In any case, it works; functional and unpretentious, this is a roll-your-sleeves-up kind of kitchen with a pleasingly unfussy air.

What catches the eye first, of course, are the red-leather-topped bar stools, which immediately say 'American diner'. You'll more often see them teamed with neon signs and rock 'n' roll memorabilia, but here they work really well to lift the look. They are suited to the space but also add a dash of quirky light-heartedness: note how they colour-coordinate with the witty 'Keep Calm and Carry On' poster.

Simplicity is often the key to designing a good kitchen (by which I mean one that not only looks good but also is convenient to work in). Here, with a fabulous walk-in larder at one end of the room, a linear layout was the obvious option, and to

preserve the essential working triangle (which should be the shape of imaginary lines drawn between fridge, sink and cooker, to make everyday activities as efficient as possible) the hob was installed in the island unit. It's a nifty solution. The cook has a choice of preparation areas; friends and family have a comfortable place to gather round and chat.

The key components of the room are, again, ultra-simple: chunky timber units, a granite worktop, the aforementioned white tiles and a two-tone linoleum floor, the shades of which perfectly complement those of the timber and stone. There's nothing ornate here; it's all about clean lines, strong shapes and a limited number of colours. This is the kitchen of an acclaimed interior designer, but it shows what can be achieved when you pare things down to the essentials and eliminate anything complex or showy. It seems to me that, when you come to think of it, nearly all great design has to do with simplicity. Less is more, as they say.

KEY FEATURES

Factory-style metal pendants are brilliantly simple and highly practical, ideal over a work surface.

Red-leather-topped bar stools add an eye-catching element of diner style to this otherwise simple, functional space.

PALE AND INTERESTING

A neutral palette provides the essentials
for this clean-lined home office, but
it's the flashes of colour that add
interest and personality.

Opposite: The bright-red chair brings liveliness and interest to an otherwise largely neutral room.

Right: The owner's beautiful ceramics are vividly coloured.

Far right: White walls and clean-lined furniture provide a calm backdrop for a selection of inspirational images.

For creativity to flourish we all have individual requirements: some people find order in chaos, others need clear space in which to think. In this serene home office there's a feeling of control and discipline, without edging into formality or constraint. The basics are minimal: a scrubbed, pale pine floor, exposed wooden beams, large, bare windows and white-painted walls. Inexpensive, attractive and neutral, these provide a blank canvas for the more colourful displays. Those consist of a variety of much-loved and indispensable items, from piles of books to artworks, and from shelves of ceramics to a wall covered with small postcards, photographs and cuttings, all of which provide essential inspiration for the owner, a ceramicist, whose vividly coloured work (made in a separate studio) is also on show.

The furniture is an eclectic mix of pieces, some old, some new, some mid-century modern, chosen with function in mind first and foremost, as should always be the case with workspaces. The huge, plain desk, comfortable office chair and capacious shelving are nothing if not practical, yet that's not to sacrifice style; their proportions are elegant, and even the office chair – an item that can be perfectly hideous – is good-looking. The extra seating fits the pared-down, natural-wood 'Scandi' look perfectly, and the adjustable desk lamp, with its elegantly geometric forms, is a subtly striking choice. But it's the addition of a design classic, the Eames DSR Eiffel-base chair in strong tomato red, that is really brilliant. It creates a focal point that lifts the room and adds a witty touch of delightful individuality. It's cool and confident, and it just shows how easy it is to mix things up to great effect.

KEY FEATURES

Easy to stick up and take down, a collection of cuttings adds decorative colour and interest, as well as providing inspiration for your work.

Simple wooden boards, pale and scrubbed, make a delightful and practical floor in virtually any room.

FANTASTIC PATTERN

In a room filled with colour and pattern,
it's essential that everything has its rightful
place. Neat piles of gorgeous retro fabrics
are all the decoration required in this
delightful home studio.

15

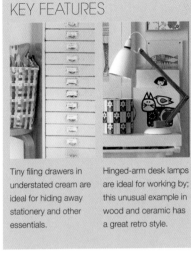

Tiny filing drawers in understated cream are ideal for hiding away stationery and other essentials.

Hinged-arm desk lamps are ideal for working by; this unusual example in wood and ceramic has a great retro style.

They say that you should choose a house based on location, location and location, but once you get inside it's storage, storage and storage that counts. Without good storage you'll be surrounded by clutter, and instead of its being a haven, your home will simply be a horrible mess. Nowhere is that more true than in a home workspace, where it's crucial to set things up so that you can find everything easily, work efficiently and feel clear-headed and comfortable. Some people prefer cupboards with doors, so that all their gear can be kept hidden away, and that is usually preferable in a home office that's part of, say, a living room or bedroom. The advantages of open-fronted storage, however, particularly in a dedicated workspace, are that you know instantly

where everything is, and – if your working materials are attractive in themselves – you have the benefit of instant, ready-made decoration around you.

This appealing home studio belongs to a screen-print and textile artist who uses vintage fabric for her work. Neatly folded and stacked on rows of shelves, the brightly coloured fabric is better than any wallpaper and looks fabulous against plain white walls. The furniture, also mostly white, is a mix of inexpensive chain-store pieces and design classics from the 1950s and 1960s, and works perfectly with the overall scheme. This bold, beautiful look is simple but extremely effective, and is guaranteed to brighten anyone's working day.

Opposite: Plain white walls and furniture are an ideal backdrop for bold colour and pattern.

Above, left: Cheap to buy and install, open shelves make great storage. But because their contents are on full display, tidiness, as here, is essential.

Above, right: Simple, colourful retro and retro-inspired designs are the unifying factor in this appealing workspace.

GIRLY GLAMOUR

Gold wallpaper and pink chenille contrast wonderfully with traditional architecture in this stunning farmhouse.

16

Left: Period architectural features combine with modern boudoir glamour to create a striking and delightful space.

Opposite: What could be more sumptuous than a gold-covered wall? This is fabulous combined with mirrored furniture and pink-and-gold fabric.

When combining old and new, it's always best to approach the task with confidence. What better example could there be than this striking bedroom, which mixes a *Sex and the City*, girl-about-town, boudoir look with rugged farmhouse architecture? This room is definitely no shrinking violet: for a start, the bare, structural timbers and high, steeply sloping ceiling are strong features in themselves. But instead of decorating in traditional country style for easy coordination, the owner has taken a bolder stance, and opted for a selection of funky, contemporary furnishings that make an instantly appealing, highly feminine statement.

Wallpaper can transform a room, providing the basis for an overall look and, as in this case, creating instant wow-factor.

The colours used in these cushions pull the entire scheme together, linking the wall with the upholstery perfectly.

Far left: Upholstering period-style furniture with modern fabric is a great trick and always looks effective.

Below: A handy storage space for going-out shoes. The contrast of old and new couldn't be more dramatic.

Let's look at the most jaw-dropping feature first: the gold metallic wall with its floral damask pattern. It's the sort of wallpaper you might expect to find in a French *palais* rather than a converted English farmhouse, but it looks great in this context, used on one 'feature' wall rather than all over (that might be just a little too much) and combined with white-painted walls and a neutral carpet. The unusual shape of this very tall wall, which is emphasized by the eye-catching wallpaper with its ultra-large repeat, adds to the interest.

The main pieces of furniture are classic in style, but brought bang up to date with some super modern upholstery in the form of spotty and stripy pink chenille – another subversion of conventional taste. The plump pink-and-gold cushions are key pieces, linking the wallpaper with the chaise at the foot of the bed, while the drum-shaped lampshades cleverly echo their colour and pattern. The bedside tables are another effective touch, their curvy legs complementing the shapes of the other furniture, and their fabulously fashionable mirrored look matching the sheen of the wall behind.

Finally, the cowhide rug, which in any room adds a confidently unconventional note (as well as a coarser texture to layer with smoother elements), is perfect here, both tonally and aesthetically. All in all, this room clashes its period architectural features with eclectic, modern pieces in a smart and savvy way.

17

HOMESPUN HEAVEN

Patchwork and crochet set the tone
for a warm, cosy guest bedroom with
a timeless air of modesty.

Tiny rooms can become jewel-like spaces when given the right treatment, and that needn't involve spending vast amounts of money; just using gorgeous colours and patterns, and furnishings that are close to your heart. Much-loved and well-worn, such pieces – particularly when they've been made by hand – have a special character, something really personal, even soulful, that contributes more to a room than any amount of money ever can.

In this sweet little guest room, for example, the two beds are covered in home-made patchwork and crochet covers. No attempt has been made to get them to match tastefully – that's not the point – and the hotchpotch of colours is delightfully vibrant, old-fashioned and yet, given the current taste for all things vintage and homespun, absolutely on-trend. Not that trends matter in the slightest here: it's all about warmth and comfort, and can't you just imagine snuggling in one of these beds, curled around a hot-water bottle, on a cold winter's night?

Adding pattern to pattern, a traditional kilim has been thrown on to the otherwise somewhat spartan floor, while a pair of unlined vintage-print curtains hangs at the window. Naïve paintings are scattered on the walls, while the distressed cupboard and a couple of wooden chairs are decidedly unmatching. It just goes to show that sometimes it is best to disregard all the 'rules' of decorating, and that a combination of inherited, home-made and junk-shop pieces can be put together in the simplest of ways to create a room with enormous appeal.

KEY FEATURES

Whether it's a crochet bedspread, a patchwork quilt or an embroidered cushion, home-made items add masses of personality.

This little chair is the simplest of pieces, the sort of thing that can be picked up for a song second hand, and looks great painted a pretty colour.

Previous page: A cacophony of colour and pattern and a selection of irresistible home-made things make this room happily homespun and charming.

Above: Using leftover paint for small items of furniture is not only thrifty but also a great way to unify a room.

Left: This crochet bedspread is simply adorable. Its unsophisticated looks work well with the traditional rug and simple, vintage-print curtains.

With busy patterns it's always wise to have a calm background, such as these cream walls.

173

THE COMFORT FACTOR

Nostalgia rules in this wallpapered
bedroom, with its laid-back mix of
vintage textiles and painted furniture.

18

For a charming, welcoming and relaxing room, you would probably not choose hard-edged, clean-lined modern furniture (effective though that can be in the right place), but rather hand-painted wood, faded fabric and old-fashioned patterns. That's exactly what the owner of this pretty bedroom has done: there is no plastic in sight, but instead blowsy florals, distressed paintwork and vintage bedlinen.

The wallpaper, a repeat of cabbage roses, is used on every wall, and really steals the show. The curtain fabric picks up its vibrant blue, as do the bed cushions, and the fabric hung below the washbasin (a great trick, this, for instant country-casual style) echoes the rose pattern but in a sunny yellow colourway. See how it all starts to work together? The bedside cupboard and an old-fashioned towel hanger are painted a matching blue but fairly bashed-about – and all the more appealing for it – while the little stool is a gorgeous pea-green, and the throw over the foot of the bed a delightful soft pink. Interestingly, not only are all these patterns from the same tonal range (which is why they work together so well), but also they're very floral. Pick a bunch of flowers from a cottage garden and this is pretty much what you'd get.

Last, but definitely not least, I must point out the plump, sprigged eiderdown, the quilted bedcover and the embroidered pillows. Rather than the duvet's modern anonymity, this traditional bed set has irresistible character and a simple look that, in keeping with the whole room, oozes comfort as well as laid-back style.

Opposite: The use of a distinctive wallpaper on every wall creates a strong atmosphere; in this case, it's one of vintage charm.

Left: A gathered panel of fabric makes a decorative disguise for storage.

Below: Try to choose accessories for their complementary colours and patterns.

KEY FEATURES

This rosy wallpaper conjures up an atmosphere of nostalgia and comfort.

These old-fashioned taps are completely in character for this room; neither too plain nor too fancy.

GEORGIAN MEETS MODERN

This room for a young boy avoids the
usual clichés by blending salvaged
furnishings with graphic prints and
bold colours.

Opposite: A salvaged bench – large, sturdy and not too precious – makes an ideal seat, with extra toy storage inside.

Right: You don't have to buy expensive, purpose-designed children's furniture; junk-shop finds can be just as good.

Hand-painted murals and fantasy beds may be just the ticket for some, but most of us decorating a child's room want value for money and a safe, functional and attractive space. Nurseries require comfort and calm, while teenagers need zones for homework and hobbies, socializing and sleepovers. In between, the priorities for a child's room, whatever its size and layout, are a comfortable bed, well-planned storage and lots of floor space for playing. While there are plenty of companies hoping to sell you an expensive, all-encompassing look, with a little individuality, lateral thinking and flair it's eminently possible to design a space that's both practical and imaginative, and doesn't cost the earth.

Take this little boy's room, for example. It's on the first floor of a city-centre Georgian terraced house, which you can just get a sense of here from its high ceilings, picture rails and bare floorboards. But there's nothing traditional about its decor. The boy's parents have avoided the conventional route of buying furniture specifically designed for children (for some reason, it seems to cost more than its adult counterparts), and instead opted for a salvaged wooden bench and a second-hand cabinet with cubbyholes. The former is a brilliant combination of seating and storage, while the latter offers masses of space to store and display books and toys while keeping them relatively well ordered. True, they could have been prettified with a lick of paint, but that's not

the look in this case. The bed, an inexpensive metal-framed job, has been jazzed up with a boldly striped throw tucked over the headboard and a mass of vividly patterned cushions, while the floor is softened for small knees with a fake cow-skin rug. Its stark black-and-white pattern is great fun, and another departure from the clichés of typical children's rooms. The finishing touch is on an otherwise unremarkable wooden armchair: on it rests a pair of cushions covered in Marimekko's signature Unikko print, its vivid crimson picking up the reds of the striking Alsatian print on the wall, and the toys and fabrics. Overall, the room is child-friendly without being childish, interesting but laid-back, cool without being overly coordinated and, importantly, easily adaptable for a growing boy.

KEY FEATURES

This bold, colourful print by Finnish design company Marimekko is fabulously funky for both adults' and children's rooms.

Good storage is essential in any child's room, and these cubbyholes are ideal for books and toys.

BATHING BEAUTY

Small is beautiful in this bathroom,
where junk-shop finds mingle with
contemporary ceramics to create
a stylish but family-friendly space.

20

It's surprising how small a bathroom can be. When designing, you can get away with a floor plan that's just as wide as a bath is long; add an adjacent handbasin and WC, and Bob's your uncle. It does help, however, if the room is beautifully fitted out: in a tiny area you'll really notice poor workmanship, and the smallest details will count for everything.

Neat tricks have been employed in this bathroom to counteract the problems that inevitably crop up in a small space. The minimal heated towel rail is wall-mounted above one end of the bath, and the bath's mixer taps and controls are also mounted in the wall, so they're sleek and unobtrusive. The backdrop is the plainest of white blinds, neutral walls, simple, stone-coloured tiles, and floorboards that appear to continue up the side of the bath. A long hanging rail is supplied for towels and dressing gowns, and there is a functional footstool. And then there's the austerely elegant rectangular basin, ultra-modern in style, that's mounted on to a fabulous junk-shop find: a prettily carved and painted antique console table that doubles as storage for all the toiletries that are best kept out of sight. This is a brilliant idea, and much more attractive than the purpose-made 'vanity units' you can buy from specialist manufacturers, although it does involve a bit of effort to get it right (ensure that the surface is at the correct height, and that the tap and waste are in the right places). What's more, the frilliness of the second-hand piece adds just the right amount of contrast with the plainer nature of everything else in the room, making this a simply irresistible combination of old and new, and another Vintage/Modern success story.

KEY FEATURES

Choose interesting towels – not terribly expensive – to introduce colour and pattern into a plain bathroom.

The pretty scalloped edges of the vintage washstand add decorative interest to this simple bathroom.

Opposite: This soft wall colour is a delightful background for the Vintage/Modern mix in this bathroom.

Above: The sleek lines of a modern basin contrast beautifully with this pretty washstand.

PURE INDULGENCE

The timeless elegance of this neutral bathroom, with classic furnishings in a modern, minimal aesthetic, makes it a luxurious, relaxing space.

21

While some people prefer brisk efficiency in a bathroom, for others the only choice is sensory seduction. It's possible to combine the two, creating a well-appointed place in which to cleanse the body as well as a haven in which to relax and recharge the mind.

As a starting point, it seems to me that a big bath really is best. There are lots of fabulous modern examples (some fabulously expensive, too, although you can find bargains if you look hard enough), but a failsafe option is the classic, roll-top, claw-footed type. It looks wonderful and fits into almost any style of scheme. In this gorgeous bathroom an Edwardian-style bath and chunky, Art Deco basin on a pedestal, with a similarly chunky chrome towel rail, make a great team. For timeless good looks – somewhere between traditional and modern, a little bit 'country' but still very chic – you can't beat tongue-and-groove woodwork around the walls; it's also useful for concealing the pipes. In this room it's painted an elegant pale brown, smart but not too sophisticated. The accessories add a lovely eclecticism, too, individual enough to be interesting but not intimidating: a frou-frou candle sconce, a completely foxed mirror and an old metal pitcher. Because they're kept to a minimum, and displayed beautifully, they have quite a strong, modern look, despite their traditional nature. A blue gingham chair seat, matching voile curtain (both of which could easily be home-made) and spotty modern toothbrush holder complete the picture, demonstrating a pulled-together thoughtfulness that makes this bathroom a truly blissful place to be.

Opposite: A selection of antique-style fittings against a cool, clean-lined background makes for a restful and luxurious room.

Right: This pretty antique wall sconce suits the room perfectly and adds great character.

Below, left: Monogrammed towels always add a touch of class.

Below, right: Against plain walls, a carefully chosen mix of antiques is highly effective.

KEY FEATURES

A heavily foxed mirror may be ineffective for checking your reflection, but it has a charming, characterful air of faded grandeur.

Tongue-and-groove wall panelling is timelessly good-looking and, in a bathroom, brilliant for concealing pipework.

DIRECTORY

COOL MODERN DESIGN

Aram
110 Drury Lane
London WC2B 5SG
+44 (0)20 7557 7557
aram.co.uk
*Modern furniture, lighting
and accessories, plus new
work by young designers*

The Conran Shop
+44 (0)8448 484000
for branches
conranshop.co.uk
*Furniture, lighting,
accessories and gifts*

Dandy Star
dandystar.com
*Groovy graphic posters,
mugs and tea towels*

Geoffrey Drayton
85 Hampstead Road
London NW1 2PL
+44 (0)20 7387 5840
and
104 High Street
Epping
Essex CM16 4AF
+44 (0)1992 573929
geoffrey-drayton.co.uk
*Furniture and lighting
from Europe's leading
designers and
manufacturers*

Histoire
Turfstraat 7a
6811 HL Arnhem
The Netherlands
+31 (0)26 3709080
histoire.nl
*Vintage and new mid-
century Modern pieces,
especially Scandinavian*

Liberty
Regent Street
London W1B 5AH
+44 (0)20 7734 1234
liberty.co.uk
*Quintessential English
emporium*

Mark
+44 (0)1326 375514
markproduct.com
*Useable, comfortable,
sustainable furniture
from Cornwall*

SCP
135–139 Curtain Road
London EC2A 3BX
+44 (0)20 7739 1869
and
87 Westbourne Grove
London W2 4UL
+44 (0)20 7229 3612
scp.co.uk
*Classic and new
furnishings that are
functional, beautiful
and made to last*

Selfridges
+44 (0)800 123400
for branches
selfridges.com
*Stylish department store
with great homeware*

Skandium
245–249 Brompton Road
London SW3 2EP
+44 (0)20 7584 2066
and
86 Marylebone High Street
London W1U 4QS
+44 (0)20 7935 2077
skandium.com
*A wide range of
Scandinavian brands*

Twenty TwentyOne
274 Upper Street
London N1 2UA
+44 (0)20 7288 1996
twentytwentyone.com
*Furniture, accessories
and lighting by
inspirational twentieth-
and twenty-first-century
designers*

RETRO AND KITSCH

Betty Boyns
2 Tregenna Hill
St Ives
Cornwall TR26 1SE
+44 (0)8450 219550
bettyboyns.co.uk
*Fabric and homeware
inspired by vintage, retro
and country themes*

Cath Kidston
+44 (0)8450 262440
for branches
cathkidston.co.uk
*Witty, reworked English
country-house style*

Greengate
+45 39 96 03 33
for branches
greengate.dk
*Pretty, nostalgic
patterned homeware*

Jane Foster Designs
janefoster.co.uk
*1960s-inspired fabric and
screen prints*

Lisa Stickley London
74 Landor Road
London SW9 9PH
+44 (0)20 7737 8067
lisastickleylondon.com
*Retro-inspired textiles,
china and linens*

SIMPLY LOVELY

ABC Carpet & Home
888 & 881 Broadway
at East 19th Street
New York, NY 10003
+1 212 473 3000
and branches in The
Bronx, New Jersey
and Florida
abchome.com
*An inspired collection of
rugs, furniture, antiques,
home textiles,
accessories and
sustainable furnishings*

Atelier Abigail Ahern
137 Upper Street
London N1 1QP
+44 (0)20 7354 8181
atelierabigailahern.com
*Quirky, cool statement
pieces*

Cox & Cox
+44 (0)8448 580734
coxandcox.co.uk
*Unusual, beautiful and
practical products by
mail order*

David Mellor
4 Sloane Square
London SW1W 8EE
+44 (0)20 7730 4259
and

The Round Building
Hathersage
Sheffield S32 1BA
+44 (0)1433 650220
davidmellordesign.com
*Kitchenware and
tableware, expertly
selected for those who
love to cook and eat*

Emma Bridgewater
+44 (0)8442 439266
for branches
emmabridgewater.co.uk
*Spongeware pottery
made in the UK*

Farrow & Ball
+44 (0)1202 876141
for stockists
farrow-ball.com
*Paints in delectable
shades and traditional
finishes*

Graham & Green
4 Elgin Crescent
London W11 2HX
+44 (0)20 7243 8908
and
164 Regents Park Rd
London NW1 8XN
+44 (0)20 7586 2960
grahamandgreen.co.uk
*Global, glamorous and
gorgeous furniture,
lighting and accessories*

i gigi General Store
31A Western Road
Hove
East Sussex BN3 1AF
+44 (0)1273 775257
igigigeneralstore.com
*A haven of beautiful gifts
and unique pieces for
the home*

Ian Mankin
271–273 Wandsworth
Bridge Road
London SW6 2TX
+44 (0)20 7722 0997
ianmankin.co.uk
*Natural and organic
fabrics, woven in the UK*

Judith Michael & Daughter
73 Regents Park Road
London NW1 8UY
+44 (0)20 7722 9000
judithmichael.com
*Brimming with antique
and vintage treasures*

Labour & Wait
18 Cheshire Street
London E2 6EH
+44 (0)20 7729 6253
labourandwait.co.uk
*Timeless, functional
products for everyday life*

Lathams
64–66 High Street
Epping
Essex CM16 4AE
+44 (0)1992 573023
and
23 North Street
Bishops Stortford
Hertfordshire CM23 2LD
+44 (0)1279 657118
lathamshome.com
*An eclectic mix
of traditional and
contemporary homeware*

Margaret Howell
34 Wigmore Street
London W1U 2RS
+44 (0)20 7009 9009
margarethowell.co.uk
*A range of new and
vintage homeware that
complements Howell's
relaxed, natural range
of clothing*

Marimekko

marimekko.com

*Finnish textiles and
wallpapers in striking,
bold patterns*

Melin Tregwynt

Castlemorris
Haverfordwest
Pembrokeshire SA62 5UX
+44 (0)1348 891288
and
26 Royal Arcade
The Hayes
Cardiff CF10 1AE
+44 (0)2920 224997
melintregwynt.co.uk

*Traditional Welsh weaving
combined with innovative,
modern design*

Neisha Crosland

+44 (0)20 7978 4389
for stockists
neishacrosland.com

*Beautiful patterned
wallpapers and fabrics*

Roger Oates

+44 (0)1531 632718
for stockists
rogeroates.com

*Classic wool flatweave
rugs and runners*

The Rug Company

therugcompany.info

*Irresistible handmade
designer rugs*

SofaSofa

Viaduct Works
Crumlin Road
Crumlin
South Wales NP11 3PL
+44 (0)1495 244226
sofasofa.co.uk

*High-quality sofas direct
from the manufacturers*

Squint

178 Shoreditch High
Street
London E1 6HU
+44 (0)20 7739 9275
squintlimited.com

*Meticulously made
upholstered furniture,
lighting and accessories,
each piece incorporating
a mix of vintage and
contemporary fabrics*

Toast

+44 (0)8445 570460
for branches
toast.co.uk

*Laid-back linens,
crockery and accessories*

The White Company

+44 (0)8456 788150
for branches
thewhitecompany.com

*Stylish, affordable,
designer-quality linens
and accessories*

CHAINS AND HIGH-STREET STORES

B&Q

+44 (0)8456 096688
diy.com

Everything for DIY

BHV

+33 (0)9 69 32 31 01
bhv.fr

*Department stores with
hardware and homewares*

Crate & Barrel

+1 800 967 6696
for branches
crateandbarrel.com

*Contemporary tableware,
kitchenware, accessories
and furniture*

Debenhams

+44 (0)8445 616161
for branches
debenhams.com

*Department store
with a strong range
of designer brands*

Habitat

habitat.co.uk

*Affordable, functional
modern design*

Home Depot

+1 800 466 3337
for branches
homedepot.com

*The world's largest home-
improvement speciality
retailer*

HomeSense

+44 (0)1923 473000
for branches
homesense.com

*Designer homewares at
up to 60 per cent off*

Ikea

ikea.com

*Affordable solutions for
better living*

John Lewis

johnlewis.com

*Everything for the home;
never knowingly undersold*

Pottery Barn

+1 888 779 5176
potterybarn.com

*Comfortable, stylish,
high-quality furnishings*

Restoration Hardware

+1 800 910 9836
restorationhardware.com

*Classic, American-style
furnishings and
decorative hardware*

SALVAGED, SECOND-HAND, RECYCLED, ANTIQUE AND ECO

After Noah

121 Upper Street
London N1 1QP
+44 (0)20 7359 4281
and
261 King's Road
London SW3 5EL
+44 (0)20 7351 2610
afternoah.com

*Unusual and interesting
antique, vintage and
contemporary furnishings*

Baileys

Whitecross Farm
Bridstow
Herefordshire HR9 6JU
+44 (0)1989 561931
baileyshomeand
garden.com

*A mix of vintage and
new that's integral to
a repair, reuse and
rethink philosophy*

BNT Antiques

47 Ledbury Road
London W11 2AA
+44 (0)20 7229 7001
bntantiques.co.uk

*Signature mirrored
pieces and other stylish
twentieth-century
antiques*

The Curtain Exchange

thecurtainexchange.co.uk

*Second-hand curtain
services, plus ready-
made and bespoke
window treatments*

Earthborn Paints

+44 (0)1928 734171
for stockists
earthbornpaints.co.uk

*Eco paints that look
sublime*

EcoBalanza

+1 888 220 6020
greenerlifestyles.com

*Sustainable and beautiful
upholstered furniture*

Ecocentric

+44 (0)800 019 7855
ecocentric.co.uk

*Beautiful, ethical, eco-
friendly interior design
products*

Fine & Dandy

The Square
Marazion
Cornwall TR17 0AP
+44 (0)1736 710611

*Hand-sewn textiles,
vintage finds and
complementary modern
accessories*

Janus

911 N. Monroe @
N. Mississippi
Portland
OR 97227
+1 503 449 5126
janushome.com

*Restored twentieth-
century furnishings
and decorative arts*

LassCo

Clergy House
Mark Street
London EC2A 4ER
+44 (0)20 7749 9944
lassco.co.uk

*Prime resource for
architectural antiques,
salvage and curiosities*

Lost City Arts

18 Cooper Square
New York, NY 10003
+1 212 375 0500
lostcityarts.com

*A leading source of
twentieth-century design
furniture, lighting and
accessories*

MascoWalcot

Cirencester Road
Aston Down
Stroud
Gloucestershire GL6 8PE
+44 (0)1285 760886
and
108 Walcot Street
Bath BA1 5BG
+44 (0)1225 444404
mascowalcot.com

*Reclaimed architectural
features and traditional
building materials*

Re

Bishops Yard
Main Street
Corbridge
Northumberland
NE45 5LA
+44 (0)1434 634567
re-foundobjects.com

*A fab mix of pieces that
are rare, remarkable,
recycled and restored*

Salvo

salvoweb.com

*Gateway to the world
of architectural salvage
and antiques*

Zwischenzeit

Raumerstr. 35
10437 Berlin
+49 (0)30 446 73371
zwischenzeit.org

*Design classics and
everyday pieces from the
1950s to the 1970s*

As always, I should like to thank my wonderful family, Martin, Felix, Tegan and Orlando, for all their help, inspiration, support and hugs. Huge thanks to the fabulous team at Merrell, who have made this book look beautiful and read wonderfully, and have also been really lovely to work with. Thanks, too, to Narratives, for working so hard to put together a superb selection of pictures, and to all the house owners who kindly let us reproduce pictures of their amazing Vintage/Modern homes.

PHOTOGRAPHY CREDITS

Caroline Arber: 63, 73, 74tr; Jan Baldwin: jacket back tl, tc, tr, c, bc, br, 2–3, 4tc, second row r, third row c, bcl, br, 5tc, second row c, third row r, 19, 20b, 25, 28b, 34–35, 43, 66r, 68, 70t, bl, br, 71br, 75, 77, 78t, b, 87, 90r, 95 second row l, third row l, br, 96tr, third row l, br, 99, second row cr, 103 t, b, 105, 106l, r, 109, 115b, 119b, 126, 127t, b, 129, 144–45, 158–59, 162–63, 171–73, 174–75, 176–77, 186; Alun Callender: 4tl, third row r, 7, 39, 61, 122b, 138–40, 146–48, 164–65, 166–67; Brent Darby: jacket back cl, 4 third row l, 5bl, 10–11, 20t, 24b, 27tl, tr, 37, 38, 48, 53, 67, 71bl, 74br, 79, 83, 84, 85, 90l, 92t, b, 95tcr, 96 second row c, 101tl, second row r, 107, 121b, 122t, 130–32, 141–43, 168–70; Jon Day: 4bl; Polly Eltes: jacket front, jacket back bl, 4 second row l, second row c, 5 second row r, third row l, third row c, br, 15, 30t, b, 33, 42t, 45, 47, 57, 71t, 95tr, bl, 96tl, second row l, bl, 98r, 100l, r, 101 second row l, br, 110b, 121t, 123b, 125r, 133–35, 149–51, 155–57, 178–79, 180–81; Tamsyn Hill: 81, 94l, r, 98l, c, 101tr, second row cl, 102, 108, 111l, r, 114 117, 120, 124; Holly Jolliffe: 136–37; Emma Lee: jacket back cr, 4bcr, 5tl, 16, 17, 54, 64, 95 second row r, third row r, 104l, 113, 116b, 118b, 123t, 125l, 182–83; Alejandro Mezza and Ezequiel Escalante: 4tr, 5tr, 12, 22, 23r, 24tr, 42b, 51, 52, 66l, 88, 91, 95tl, tcl, third row c, 96 second row r, third row c, 97, 104r, 106c, 118t, 119t; David Parmiter: 112t; Ingrid Rasmussen: 31, 41, 49, 74l, 101tc, 110t, 112b; Claire Richardson: 5 second row l, 27b, 23l, 28t, 59, 115t, 116t; Verity Welstead: 24tl, 90c, 93, 96 third row r, 152–54, 160–61.

PROJECT CREDITS

2–3, 34–35, 68, 162–63 Owner: Charlotte Crosland, charlottecrosland.com.

7, 146–48 Stylist: Fiona McCarthy. Owner: Rose Bamford, dandystar.com. 'Love' poster by Dandy Star.

10–11, 37, 79, 130–32 Stylist: Sian Williams. Owner: Lisa Stickley, lisastickleylondon.com.

15 Stylist: Gabi Tubbs. Owner: Zoe Ellison, igigigeneralstore.com.

16, 54, 116b, 123t, 125l, jacket back cr Owner: Emma Bridgewater, emmabridgewater.co.uk.

17 Owner: Ruth Corbett. 'Rubbish' rug by Vivienne Westwood, from The Rug Company. Cushions by Melin Tregwynt. 'Crisp' table from the Conran Shop.

19, 78t, b, 95br Stylist: Cathy O'Clery.

20t Stylist: Hazel Dolan. Owner: Marie McLaughlin.

20b, 129, 171–73 Owners: Stephen Rothholz and Liz Evans.

23l Stylist: Lorraine Dawkins.

24tl Stylist: Emma Marshall.

24tr Architect: Javier Gentile.

24b Stylist: Hazel Dolan. Owners: Nicola and Jason Wilson.

25, 70bl, jacket back c Owner: John Nicolson.

27tl, tr, 71bl, 74br Stylist: Hazel Dolan. Owner: Lizzie Clarke, thewoodlands-sandsend.com.

27b, 28t, 116t Owner: Hilary Lowe.

28b Owner: Lionel Copley.

30t, 33, 47, jacket back bl Owner: Abigail Ahern, atelierabigailahern.com.

30b Stylist: Gabi Tubbs. Owners: Christopher Stocks and Roy Barker.

31, 41, 49, 74l Stylist: Sarah Fry.

38, 53, 67, 168–70 Stylist: Sian Williams. Owner: Liz Hellmers.

39, 122b Stylists: Melanie Molesworth (page 39); Abigail Edwards (page 122b). Owner: Ann Louise Roswald. Walls in 'Rectory Red' and 'House White' by Farrow & Ball. Bedcover from a selection of limited-edition Ann Louise Rothwald 'archive fabric' patchwork quilts. Bathroom mural hand-painted by Ann Louise Roswald. Fashion designer Ann Louise Rothwald's rural retreat on the west coast of Ireland, annlouiseroswald.com.

42t, 45, 178–79 Stylist: Sian Williams. Owners: Fiona and Alex Cox, coxandcox.co.uk.

43 Architect: Jonathan Clark, jonathanclark.co.uk. Owner: James McNamara.

48, 122t Stylist: Hazel Dolan. Owner: Gillian Anderson Price, judithmichael.com.

52 Architect: Diego Montero.

63 Stylist: Gabi Tubbs.

66r, jacket back br Owner: Cath Kidston, cathkidston.co.uk.

70t, br, 77, 106r, jacket back bc Owner: Margaret Howell. Furniture (page 77): Lisa Whatmough, Squint.

71t Stylist: Gabi Tubbs. Owners: Sarah and Antony Parham.

73, 74tr Stylist: Gabi Tubbs.

75 Interior design: Grant White Design, grantwhitedesign.com.

81 Stylist: Sylvie Jones.

83, 84, 85 Stylist: Hazel Dolan. Owner: Alison Norris-Baber, agnescoy.co.nz.

90c, 152–54 Stylist: Emma Marshall. Owner: Wendy Lunar.

91 Architect: Diego Montero.

92t Stylist: Sian Williams. Architect: Christopher Pallis, axiadevelopment.com.

92b Stylist: Hazel Dolan. Owners: Julie and Paul Trelease.

93 Stylist: Emma Marshall.

99 Cushions by Georgina von Etzdorf, gve.co.uk.

100l Stylist: Angela A'Court.

100r Owners: Sue and Rob Reeves.

103t Owners: Peter Ting and Brian Kennedy.

103b Architect: Kay Hartmann.

106c, 119b Architect: Melloco Moore.

110t Owner: Richard Parr.

115t Stylist: Lorraine Dawkins.

115b Owners: Peter Ting and Brian Kennedy.

119t Architect: Fernando Villarino.

121b Stylist: Sian Williams. Owners: Harriet and Lachlan Campbell.

123b Stylist: Celia Rufey. Owner: Jose Strawson.

125r Stylist: Jane Graining. Owners: Nikki and Charles Wright, wrenriver.com.

126 Owners: Vicky and Simon Young.

133–35 Stylist: Gabi Tubbs. Owner: Bernadette Lewis, bntantiques.co.uk.

136–37 Architect: Keith Cunningham, coastarchitects.co.uk. Owner: vintagevacations.co.uk.

138–40 Stylist: Abigail Edwards. Owner: Lisbeth Johnson-Toivenen.

141–43 Owner: Rebecca Fishenden.

144–45, 176–77 Stylist: Cathy O'Clery. Owners: Lulu Roper-Caldbeck and Marcus James.

149–51, jacket front Stylist: Celia Rufey. Owner: Simi Bedford.

155–57 Stylist: Celia Rufey. Owner: James Cole.

158–59 Stylist: Vinny Lee. Owner: Bridget Bodoano.

160–61 Stylist: Emma Marshall. Owner: Lisa Moylett.

164–65 Owner: Bodil Manz.

166–67 Stylist: Abigail Edwards. Owner: Jane Foster, janefoster.co.uk.

174–75, jacket back tc Stylist: Mary Norden. Owner: Victoria Stapleton, brora.co.uk.

180–81 Stylist: Celia Rufey. Owner: Jose Strawson.

Jacket back tl Stylist: Cathy O'Clery. Owners: Rhonda Drakeford and Harry Woodrow.

First published 2011 by

Merrell Publishers Limited
81 Southwark Street
London SE1 0HX

merrellpublishers.com

British Library Cataloguing-in-Publication data:
Sorrell, Katherine.
The vintage/modern home.
1. Antiques in interior decoration. 2. Used furniture. 3. Found objects (Art)
in interior decoration. 4. Interior decoration accessories. 5. New and old.
I. Title
747-dc22

ISBN 978-1-8589-4527-9

Produced by Merrell Publishers Limited
Designed by Alexandre Coco
Project-managed by Rosanna Lewis
Indexed by Hilary Bird

Printed and bound in Shenzhen

Merrell Publishers is grateful to the premium rights-managed interiors and
lifestyle photographic agency Narratives for providing the photographs
published in this book. Founded in 1999, Narratives provides a specialist
resource for contemporary features and imagery on the theme of the home,
including such subjects as homes and gardens, interior decoration, still life,
places to stay and day-to-day living, as well as seasonal themes and inspiring
incidental details. Narratives is a member of the British Association of Picture
Libraries and Agencies (BAPLA).
narratives.co.uk; +44 (0)20 3137 3739